RESILIENCE
BETWEEN PAIN AND PURPOSE
featuring The Growth Codes

Marlon Rollins, PhD, LMHC, LPCC

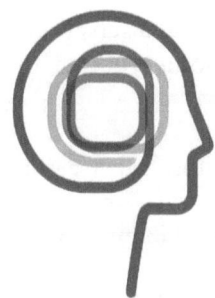

Mind Transformed, LLC
www.drmarlonrollins.com

Resilience: Between Pain and Purpose
featuring the Growth Codes
by Dr. Marlon Rollins, LMHC, LPCC

Copyright © 2025

All rights reserved. No part of this book may be reproduced or used in any manner without written permission of the copyright owner except for the use of quotations in book reviews or other limited non-commercial uses.

This book is a work of non-fiction and is based on real events, observations, and experiences. Some names, identifying details, and locations have been changed or fictionalized to respect the privacy of individuals and organizations. Any resemblance to actual persons, living or deceased, or to real events is purely coincidental. The content of this book is intended for informational and reflective purposes only and should not be considered professional advice.

Although the publisher and the author have made every effort to ensure that the information in this book was correct at press time and while this publication is designed to provide accurate information in regard to the subject matter covered, the publisher and the author assume no responsibility for errors, inaccuracies, omissions, or any other inconsistencies herein and hereby disclaim any liability to any party for any loss, damage, or disruption caused by errors or omissions, whether such errors or omissions result from negligence, accident, or any other cause.

This publication is meant as a source of valuable information for the reader, however it is not meant as a substitute for direct expert assistance. If such level of assistance is required, the services of a competent professional should be sought.

Editor: Lyda Carrillo

Copyright filed with Library of Congress, June 2025

ISBN: 979-8-9990077-0-4

"You may encounter many defeats, but you must not be defeated.

In fact, it may be necessary to encounter the defeats, so you can know who you are, what you can rise from, and how you can still come out of it."

Dr. Maya Angelou

This book is dedicated to Mrs. Gina Tabrizy. My dear friend, *sister* and nurturer. Thank you for seeing me. You touched so many lives profoundly and went home on January 24, 2025. You will not be forgotten.

"I stand at the precipice of life. A voice calls to the longing in my soul. Be not afraid to jump, you can fly! When all that you know is gone and all that you have is the certainty of nothing, there will all things become possible."

Gina Tabrizy, LMFT

Table of Contents

Introduction
Resilience Required   i

Chapter 1
The Pain, Process and Purpose -
The Bounce Back: December 31, 2013   1

Chapter 2
To CEO or Not CEO   8

Chapter 3
Take the Journey   16

Chapter 4
The Codes for Growth   107

References   155

Introduction

Resilience Required

We all experience suffering, misfortune and uncertainty in life. These times can leave us feeling broken, disoriented and wondering why we are even here. We encounter difficulties that push us beyond our comfort zones and compel us to explore the darkest parts of our psyche.

You may have heard the phrase "There is purpose in our pain," but how do we arrive at purpose from the pain? How do we get from here to there; from hurt to hope? What is the road map from these dark places? How do we transition our wounding griefs, shames, heartbreaks and losses into something that has meaning? This book is all about how you can make that transition from pain into purpose.

We have, during times of adversity, a crucial option that has the power to change the path of our lives. We may give in to the pressure of our suffering and let it define us, or we can conjure a fortitude that turns our anguish into a source of power and motivation. How do you want to respond to adversity?

In *Resilience: Between Pain and Purpose* I take you with me on a transformational journey across the tapestry of my personal and professional experiences. This book is an investigation of the areas where suffering, process and purpose converge, shedding light on the fundamental and frequently elusive relationship between them. Purpose is the manifestation of pain that's been overcome. When we live into purpose it is not only our story — it becomes our legacy. Our legacy is the impact on the environment we will live in. It is a signal of our eternal energy.

In *Resilience*, we'll learn about the possibility for change, the extraordinary fortitude of the human spirit and the gap between the depths of suffering and the zeniths of purpose. I ask you to consider resilience not just as a character trait but as a dynamic response to tragic events in life. We'll look at methods for conquering challenges, finding courage in the face of hopelessness and releasing the amazing power that lives inside each of us. You may be familiar with *Post Traumatic Growth* (Dell'Osso, et al, 2022). In summation, this work presents the idea that there exists in a traumatic event the potential for positive-growth. Getting on the other side of a life crisis, years of neglect, chronic stress or emotional abuse is a precarious journey from survival into living at a higher level. If we are unable to wrestle the adaptive protective mechanism at work we can lose sight of ourselves in the pain. This book also offers what I refer to as the Growth Codes, which are the elements you can use to build an internal framework for fulfillment and success. They are a way to get from pain into purposeful living.

Join me on a journey from pain into purpose. Along the way, I ask you also to examine you own journey of transformation. We investigate the facets of resilience; the physical, emotional, relational and the spiritual. I share personal and professional insights as a guide on this journey of purposeful living. This trip offers motivation, encouragement and the awareness that there is always a way to find the light, no matter how dark things may seem. This book is designed to help you to create your own road map to the other side of uncertainty.

Are you prepared to experience resilience's transformational power? If yes, let's set out on this trip from affliction to meaning together — a journey that could permanently alter how you view both your own life and the world in which you live.

How do we emerge when life feels it is collapsing in on us? When all that we have worked for seems to be crumbing away? All we want is for things to go back to normal or to simply be okay. But normal places are a far distance away now, the places we are in are dark and there's no apparent light at the end of the tunnel because we are in too deep, and our vision is not adapted to these places. Or we fear the light in the tunnel is another train to run us down. These are the moments in time when we can become hopeless. There are many who get stuck in these dark places and with these thoughts. You don't have to be one of them if you grasp what to do in these places of pain and uncertainty.

Author Joseph Campbell famously said, "We must let go of the life we have planned so as to accept the one that is waiting for us." Master storytellers weave the common plot of the unwitting hero who is well-intended with the pursuit of happiness and with their own vague ideas of how the journey of life should play out; set with well-orchestrated milestones of health, wealth and family. Similarly, from childhood we frequently design a blueprint — a magnificent vision for our lives from adults' words uttered to us "What do you want to be when you grow-up?" It is surely an inspiring question for the innocent mind with unlimited creativity but with limited wisdom. We set sail with hopes, plans and well-planned routes. It's as if we're embarking on a journey to higher heights; assured of our destination and steadfast in our path.

Yet, in its infinite wisdom, life has a way of surprising us: changing our futures and guiding us into unexplored seas. We face storms that put our fortitude to the test — as well as diversions that put our beliefs to the test. We are presented with a fundamental option in these moments of divergence from the script.

To "let go of the life we've planned" implies that we let go of our fixed ideas about how our path ought to unfold. It's an admission that the screenplay we've written may not always correspond with the complicated story true life has in store for us. It's a surrendering act from the lesson that the artistry of life is frequently found in its unpredictability.

As you read or listen, I want you to yield to the idea of a way out. Catch yourself and take note of thoughts that come to your mind that bring discomfort. Surrender to the present moment and recognize these as opportunities to transform. In the first portion of the book, I will take you on my own healing path, both personally and professionally. Center to the book is understanding the aspects of resilience. The elements in between our pain and our purpose are where people tend to get lost. There is much more uncertainty in the between. These crises are pivotal points that can change the trajectory of our journey. However, we are limited in our capacity to cope in those moments and we tend to react in fear. Therefore, the latter portion of the book is intended to serve as a guide to help you navigate your own life adversities and transform them from meaning to active purpose.

Resilient Communities

As I write this book, the Palisades and Eaton wildfires are raging through communities in Southern California. These fires remain uncontained; their destructive force unrelenting. From my driveway I can see smoke billowing over the hills — a stark reminder of the fragility of life and the suddenness with which adversity can strike. I am soberly grateful that my family and me are safe, but my heart aches for those who have lost so much. Amid this devastation, one word keeps surfacing in news broadcasts and community discussions: resilience.

Resilience is often invoked in times of crisis, yet it is not something that materializes out of thin air. It is not attained in a vacuum or by sheer willpower alone. Resilience is forged in the crucible of experience and discovered through the resounding response to hardship. It is a process—a journey that unfolds through action, connection and compassion.

During these wildfires I have seen countless acts of response. Emergency personnel risk their lives to rescue families and contain the flames. Neighbors open their homes to those who have been displaced. Volunteers distribute food, water and blankets to those in need. These actions go beyond thoughts and prayers; they are tangible expressions of care and solidarity. Each act of kindness — no matter how small — contributes to the collective resilience of the community.

Resilience requires more than just action: it necessitates safety and compassion. In the aftermath of unexpected adversity people are vulnerable—physically, emotionally and spiritually. The road to resilience begins with acknowledging this vulnerability and creating spaces where individuals can feel safe and supported. Safety is not just about physical protection from harm; it is about fostering an environment where people can process their pain, share their stories and begin to heal.

Compassion for others builds a bridge between pain and purpose. It is the catalyst that transforms suffering into strength and despair into hope. Compassion fuels the response to adversity, reminding us that we are not alone. When communities come together in compassion, they create a foundation for resilience to emerge. Compassion doesn't erase the pain; it gives it meaning. It transforms the narrative from one of mere survival to one of purpose and growth.

Resilience, then, is not a static trait but a dynamic process. It is built through cycles of challenge, response, and recovery. It is the collective effort of individuals and communities to face hardship with courage and to rebuild with intention. The wildfires have reminded us that resilience is as much about what we do for one another as it is about what we endure. It is a testament to the human spirit's capacity to rise above adversity and to find renewed purpose even in the ashes of devastation.

Developing resilience in individuals and communities requires intentional methods that foster growth and adaptability. For individuals, this means cultivating a mindset of optimism, learning from past experiences and building strong social connections. Practices such as gratitude, emotional expression, and asking for help are critical tools in developing personal resilience. Engaging in meaningful activities and setting realistic goals also help individuals find purpose — even in difficult times.

Communities that demonstrate higher resilience often exhibit strong networks of support and a culture of mutual aid. These communities invest in preparedness, ensuring that systems and structures are in place to respond effectively to crises. Education and awareness campaigns help residents understand potential risks and empower them to take proactive steps. Inclusive leadership and equitable resource distribution are also crucial, as they ensure that no one is left behind during recovery efforts.

Ultimately, resilience is built through a combination of individual and collective efforts. By fostering a culture of compassion, safety, and preparedness, we can equip ourselves and our communities to not only withstand adversity but to emerge stronger and more united in its aftermath.

Chapter 1

The Pain, Process and Purpose - The Bounce Back: December 31, 2013

*F*OLLOWING MY SISTER AMBER'S DEVASTATING SUICIDE, I found myself on the verge of an irrevocably altered existence. A tidal wave of trauma had flooded through our family tree, leaving us all profoundly distraught — just like the numerous people Amber had impacted in her all-too-brief journey.

The issue that plagued us — and that I struggled with both as her brother and as an experienced clinician — was the relentless question: "Why?" Why did this happen, and could we have changed the outcome? "Why" is a childlike question we all ask when faced with the incomprehensible. Yet, the answer rarely lies in the *why*. Dwelling on the *why* leaves us spinning in the corners of a dark room, searching for clarity that never comes. A more useful question is, "How do I move through this?" But before we can find our way forward, we must first understand how something makes us feel. We should understand the energy of the events. We must allow ourselves to fully experience its impact.

But there was another concern that weighed heavily on my mind, one that I, as a brother and a therapist, couldn't avoid. It was the terrible thought of what else I could have done. I had last seen her five days before she slipped away from us. Her eyes bore the marks of her internal fight, and the exhaustion of her spirit was obvious. As her brother it troubled me.

Instead of confronting the elephant in the room, the terrifying prospect of suicidal thoughts, I deviated into lighter territory, telling experiences and cracking jokes until the room resonated with laughter. Was that a quiet farewell as she engulfed me in that painful, prolonged hug? The fact is that I had no idea. All I knew was that my presence had brought her solace, but it had been insufficient to combat the darkness that engulfed her in her last moments.

I became lost in a web of shame as I navigated the tumultuous rivers of my own sorrow, struggling with the unfathomable complexity of her loss. My reflection provided no relief; instead; it served as a constant reminder of the stone of agony that had settled deep within.

In my search for answers and understanding, I switched my gaze outside, scrutinizing the plethora of factors that had surrounded her, the pressures that had influenced her path to seek help.

The weight of stigma, the onerous load of exposing one's issues with drug addiction and bipolar depression, had thrown a long, dark shadow over her. The challenges to excellent care she encountered, as well as the constraints imposed by the intricate maze of health insurance, were insurmountable obstacles on her road to recovery. As if that weren't enough, her work as a nurse, her lifeline through which she had committed herself to helping others, had now become a casualty of her struggle. The suspension of her nursing license just added to her sense of isolation while the help she so needed remained elusive.

Amber's path and tragic conclusion sparked a profound shift in me. It ignited a burning desire to rewrite the narrative around mental health, substance misuse, and the unsung tragedies of many people. Her story — one of struggle, misery, and ultimately, unfathomable loss — has become my unshakeable motivation to make a difference. In her memory I wanted to dismantle the barriers that prevented her from receiving the care she needed and ensure that others do not endure the same silent agony.

Yet, in my efforts to address these external barriers I neglected to initially tend to the deeper impact her loss had on me. It was like watching a heavy stone drop into water: we notice the sound, the splash and the rippling waves, but rarely do we consider the stone itself, sinking below the surface. As it descends, it displaces everything around it, altering the depths in ways we cannot immediately see. While I focused on the waves — the outward ripples of her story — I overlooked the quiet, profound shifts taking place within me; the subtle but deep changes left in the stone's wake.

I saw clearly that more could have been done during her treatment. During her first psychiatric hospitalization in April 2013, she had to self-report her drug use to the Indiana State Nursing Assistance Program (ISNAP), an agency under the Board of Nursing that aids nurses with substance use issues. They estimate that up to 6% of nurses in the state will struggle with substance use problems. Now, my sister was counted among them. She had so much pride and purpose in being a nurse, but the label of addiction brought her deep shame. The stigma drove her into a deeper depression. The notion of being proud to help others but unable to help herself was a spear to her soul.

On the outside she had a bright, beautiful smile that energized everyone she encountered. But depression and grief, as it does, pulled at her mind and heart, dragging her into emotional agony.

Leading up to Amber's death, she was enrolled in an Intensive Outpatient Program (IOP), attending group sessions three times a week as part of her probationary requirement to participate in a substance abuse treatment program. However, I questioned the quality of the support she received. It didn't seem like she was getting real help — just checking a box so the program could bill her insurance. This became painfully evident when she ended her life. Her journal was filled with self-deprecating words: "What's wrong with me? Why can't I stop?" These were cries of desperation. Yet, no safety plan or suicide risk assessment seemed to have been in place. Was anyone even asking if she had access to a gun? What was actually being addressed in her group or individual sessions?

After she died, I meticulously reviewed the records she kept in a plastic and vinyl file folder — the same room where she took her last breath. She had received letters denying her Medicaid coverage and had even applied for disability, only to receive a lengthy rejection stating that her condition wasn't severe enough. The letter cited her college education, recent manual labor work, and the fact that she hadn't been impaired for over twelve months. Thirteen days before her death, she received a letter from the State Nursing Board deeming her "unfit to practice due to impairment." The correspondence documented her struggles since her hospitalization in April, even noting that she had been homeless. Following her divorce earlier that year, her life had spiraled into crisis. The very systems meant to support her had instead pushed her through another crack.

After her death, nothing changed at the health-care agency where she had sought treatment. It was business as usual. When I reached out, their response was shockingly indifferent — as if they had come to expect these tragic losses. I was met with a cold, "I'm sorry for your loss." It felt like a passive insult, something I had to swallow. Instead of soothing me it ignited my grief into something sharper.

Adding to the insult, I had once worked for the same organization. I remembered my first weeks of orientation, where new hires met with the CEO. I had been impressed that he took the time to sit with us, share the organization's vision, and personally engage with new staff. He invited us to ask questions, presiding at the head of the boardroom table.

As a researcher and inquisitive employee, I focused my questions on preventative health. Given that he oversaw the largest mental health program in our town, I assumed he would have valuable insights on prevention. His response was immediate and unequivocal: "There is no money in prevention." He offered no further explanation. The message was clear: profit took precedence over helping the community. That answer never sat well with me, and I left the company a year later for a better opportunity.

In the wake of my sister's death, I saw with painful clarity that the organization's mission had never been about getting her life back on track or even keeping her safe. Instead, the goal seemed to be keeping her in therapy for as long as possible to maximize billing. As long as she was insured, she had value. Once she was gone, she was no longer a source of revenue.

For those of us left behind, the loss was immeasurable. I had lost a sister. A mother lost her daughter. A daughter lost her mother. Her friends lost a cherished companion. Her patients lost a compassionate nurse. The community lost a dedicated healthcare worker — forever.

This profit-driven strategy raises serious concerns about the mental health system, particularly for those with mood and thought disorders. Navigating treatment ought not feel like solving a maze. If profit is the primary motivation, then the goal is not recovery but retention — keeping clients dependent on services rather than truly helping them heal.

In other areas of medicine, preventative care is common practice. Routine screenings for cancer and other diseases are standard when reaching certain age milestones. However, mental health is rarely approached with the same proactive mindset. If you receive psychological screenings at your primary care visits, consider yourself fortunate. Many struggle just to access health-care in the first place.

On a larger scale, we have failed to view mental health through a preventative lens. The prison system remains the largest provider of mental health services in the U.S. According to the National Alliance on Mental Illness (NAMI), over 60% of individuals in prison who require mental health treatment still do not receive it. Even within the prison system, the goal is containment — not rehabilitation.

We know enough today about brain development, high-risk populations, and vulnerable professions to take a proactive approach to behavioral health-care. Without clients or patients, there is no business — that's understandable. But an organization's response to the death or suffering of those in its care reflects its true values. Every loss of life ought to prompt a critical examination of service delivery. The next person who walks through the door deserves better.

My sister's tragic story has not only reshaped my mission but also redefined my values and purpose. Her struggle fuels my determination to create systemic change. I am committed to advocating for better mental health-care, reducing stigma and promoting preventive measures.

Chapter 2

To CEO or Not CEO

AS I NAVIGATE THIS NEW CHAPTER, I INVITE YOU, the reader, to reflect on your role in this journey. In many respects we are CEOs of our own lives. We can create vision and a plan for where we want to be. We bring our values and morals to guide us through. How can we collectively break down the barriers that prevent people from receiving quality behavioral health-care? This also includes supports you would want to seek out for yourself. Together, we can honor the memory of those we've lost by creating a more compassionate and effective system.

After going to therapy and doing grief work, I felt courageous enough to begin to share Amber's story and my experience as her brother at work. The health-care organization I worked for was awarded the *Zero Suicide initiative* through a SAMHSA federal grant. Over two million dollars was awarded to our organization to help invest in creating an integrated system design to help reduce suicides. It was the first time I saw the potential power in storytelling and investing in treatment enhancement and care coordination. It gave me the sense that maybe her death did not have to be in vain. That I might use her loss, and my loss of her, to open the hearts of others to listen beyond the stigma of addiction and mental health conditions. It was no longer just about protocols and systems but about creating a more empathetic and connected group of people working together for a shared purpose.

After a year of working on the project with our healthcare team, in 2015 I was invited to speak at the National Council of Behavioral Health, now called the National Council of Mental Wellness (NatCon). The conference is regarded as the largest mental health and substance use treatment conference in the world. I remember the late Colin Powell was slotted to be a main keynote that year. I was there to speak in a breakout session on behavioral health integration in primary care and highlight crisis services and the work we were doing to enhance care delivery with our employer.

I was thrilled to represent our company at this forum. Prior to the start of the main conference, there was a pre-conference of special sessions. One of those sessions was entitled "To CEO or not CEO." The session was led by an experienced recruiter who would help hospitals find fit CEOs to lead their organization. During the session he went over attributes that were key traits that "make a good CEO." Things like being a good listener, having a clear vision, the ability to communicate with others, being a multi-tasker and strategic planner and having patience as well as financial acumen.

In addition to his overview of the characteristics and recruiting process, there was also a question-and-answer session with a handful of current and former CEOs who shared their words of wisdom and obstacles.

As the session continued, my boss at the time, the vice president of the Behavioral Health Hospital, turned and whispered to me, "Marlon, that sounds like you." Her words affirmed what I had already been sensing without saying it aloud. Job titles seemed to be all the rave. The appeal of being a CEO gave me enthusiasm. I knew, even from this session, that the title and authority came with tremendous responsibility — not only for the well-being of clients and patients but also for the workforce. Nonetheless, I saw it as a position where I could make a significant impact. Being a CEO could allow me to shape the right mission in the industry — a mission focused on quality and service. Peeking through this new door of purpose gave me a sense of new possibility. The question remained: how would I get from here to there?

At the time, I was a director of operations for both the crisis department and the inpatient psychiatric hospital. Nearly two years after my sister's death, we had made significant enhancements, including facility remodels, training initiatives, new protocols, job roles and operational systems. I worked tirelessly with the team to create a better patient experience at every level. That same year, a job opportunity opened for an executive director role. I saw it as my chance to take the next step and build upon the progress we had made. But the job went to someone else — someone with less tenure than I had. I was frustrated. What more could I have done? I had the degrees, the licenses, the experience. Why was I not chosen? Again, I defaulted to the "why" question, but I needed to accept the reality. The response was, "wait for the next opportunity."

But there was no clear path forward. Senior leaders had been with the company for decades, and waiting for someone to retire was not a viable succession plan. I had invested deeply in the organization, yet it felt unreciprocated — like a one-sided relationship where my contributions were acknowledged but not truly valued.

I came to a resolution: when one door closes, others will open. Sometimes, you must seek out better doors if the ones you knock on refuse to open. My pursuit became clear: I needed to find an opportunity that would develop me further. I took it as a sign to move.

Leaving Indiana became an increasingly ideal plan. The pain had served its purpose: it had moved me beyond my comfort zone. Now, it was time to choose myself and my purpose.

In my search for greater opportunities — spaces of warmth, development, and healing — I cast a wide net. My focus shifted to California, where my sister had always wanted to live. I was drawn to the West Coast by recollections of a prior vacation to Southern California and the promise of reconnecting with half-siblings and undiscovered relatives. It appeared to be an opportunity to solve the mystery surrounding my biological father's origins.

During my several health-care job searches, I came upon an intriguing position in Fremont, California. The employment comprised training as a chief operating officer (COO) for a for-profit behavioral health corporation, with the eventual objective of becoming a CEO supervising behavioral health institutions countrywide. This looked to be the ideal chance for me. I got an in-person interview after an arduous application procedure. I took a few days off in the spring of 2016 to research and interview for the role. The employment was in a 148-bed psychiatric inpatient hospital in the Bay Area. The warmth of the California sun greeted me as I arrived to the new city. I was soon rejected from the application procedure because I didn't have the financial backing they were looking for to move forward. But the CEO of the facility advocated on my behalf, believing I had the character and potential to be good fit. I got the job.

Recognizing our shortcomings and accepting the likelihood of mistakes is a universal human experience. Each of us is confronted with foreseeable limitations and inherent flaws. Paradoxically, it is precisely within these flaws that the opportunity for great human development exists. Indeed, the infusion of divine favor acts as a sobering reminder that our genuine way ahead stretches beyond our own achievements. As demonstrated in the paradox of being viewed as unqualified yet getting access to where one genuinely belongs, believing in one's absolute right owing to earned merit can mistakenly lead to the rejecting of chances. This paradox reveals the transformative power of grace, a divine influence that outperforms our human efforts and inspires us to retain unshakable faith.

This experience emphasizes an important lesson: regardless of our scars and shortcomings, grace has the power to open doors designed for us. To accept grace, one must first extend it to oneself — a critical step in discovering one's mission. It exemplifies the transformational power of embracing shortcomings, allowing grace to pervade our lives and acknowledging that our journey is ultimately directed by powers beyond our immediate control.

In times of uncertainty, stand up and believe in the grace that might unfold, embracing both the difficulties and the possibility of new beginnings. If you are wondering if you have what it takes, you are at a transition point of exiting your comfort zone towards growth.

Battling Insecurity

Take a moment to reflect or even write down answers to the questions below. When we are shifting into a new place or opportunity, it is common to doubt ourselves. Answering these questions can help better equip you for what is ahead to help us shift.

1. What fears arise when you think about stepping into a new challenge or opportunity?

2. What past experiences have shaped your beliefs about your ability to grow and succeed?

3. In what ways do you seek external validation, and how does it impact your confidence?

4. What internal narratives or self-doubts tend to surface when you're about to step into new territory?

5. How do you typically respond to discomfort or uncertainty — do you embrace it, resist it or avoid it?

6. What limiting beliefs have you carried that no longer serve you at this stage of growth?

7. Are there patterns of self-sabotage or procrastination that emerge when you feel challenged?

8. What strengths or past victories can you draw upon to reassure yourself during this transition?

9. Who in your life supports your growth, and how can you lean on them for encouragement?

10. What is a truth about yourself that makes you more confident to move forward?

11. What is one courageous step you can take today to lean into your growth instead of into your insecurities?

NOTES

Chapter 3

Take the Journey

Setting out for California and venturing into an unfamiliar landscape was reminiscent of Joseph Campbell's Call to Adventure in *The Hero's Journey*. I understood that this was more than simply a career switch; it was a life-altering decision, a door opening to further opportunities and the ability to help others on another level.

The job started on July 5th, which was also the anniversary of a life-transforming miracle. Three years prior, I had donated a kidney to my chosen father. It solidified his role of father in my life, in the absence of my biological father. It was a compelling reminder of the cyclical nature of life and the possibility of new beginnings.

Simultaneously, I also carried pieces of my sister's loss and pain with me on this journey. There was no escaping that grief. But rather than letting these feelings hinder me, I decided to use them as forces for transformation. Though my sister's life had ended, I felt compelled to continue and add the meaning of her life to my own journey. In that way, she was still with me, even though her journey had ended sooner than expected. I had to carry on with her in a different way.

I gave my present company a two-week notice of my resignation as July 5thth drew near. They had asked for a month, but I agreed to give them an extra week to provide any hand-off information to aid in the transfer of duties. In my heart, I sensed that my time there had come to an end; it was more than just a change of employment. It was the end of one part of my journey, but I was taking with me the lessons learned. With my sister now gone, she was my soul connection to the place where we grew up. We had dreamed of leaving, so this was also in honor of her hopes. Nevertheless, there were moments of anger that she had ended her life and was not here to share this journey with me. I felt like she was missing out. Ahead now was a chance for personal healing, professional advancement, and a deeper realization of my purpose.

The trip came to pass with a planned week-long road journey from Indiana to California, where I said goodbye to one chapter and welcomed the next. I booked an Airbnb for my arrival, with the intention of moving my chosen father to California and helping him locate a decent apartment, thereby starting a new chapter in both of our lives. I broke the trip up into four segments, each of approximately eight-hours, to give myself enough time to rest and allow me to explore each destination a bit. I loaded my BMW convertible coupe with as much as I could.

I believed my car was meant to be in California. My 2010 BMW was black with a coral red interior with paddle shifters and nineteen-inch rims with the sport package. It was a rare find car that got your attention when the hard top folded down like a transformer. The interior color felt like passion on wheels with the sound to match. The plan was to travel from Indianapolis, Indiana, to Kansas City, Kansas, to Denver, Colorado, to Las Vegas, Nevada, and finally arrive in San Jose, California, by the weekend.

The cross-country trip was also a bucket list item, and I decided to focus on the journey rather than the destination. Time alone on the road gave me space to reflect on the past, enjoy the present moment, and think about the possibilities ahead. Embarking on this road trip, my first stop was Kansas City. The main draw to Kansas was all about the barbeque. Smoked meat and sweet, savory sauces put the pin on my map. It is fascinating how setting a simple goal can drive you. I knew well that this would be my exit from Indiana with no looking back. There was no better way to make the first leg of the trip than by enjoying a rack of ribs, baked beans, pulled pork, and mac and cheese. I didn't plan any other details except the destination: barbeque. There is something about over-planning that can choke out other possibilities and narrow our vision. The highway gave direction and speed was my timeframe.

Another curious element of this first leg of the trip was that Kansas City, Kansas, was also the birthplace of my biological father. Though he was estranged from my sister and me from a young age, his mysterious life and death intrigued us. Frankly, I didn't understand his plight in life; I only experienced how parts of it impacted my sister and me. His absence from our lives left unanswered questions. Until he died in early 2013, just before my sister ended her life, we had hoped to see him again. With them both gone, it was only me now for this journey. The first stop symbolized not only a transition in my career but also the exploration of my origin — a return home I had never visited. From what I knew, my father's family left their hometown in the Midwest for greater opportunities out West. In fact, my father spent a significant amount of time in California and the Bay Area, which was where I was ultimately headed.

How else can we break patterns if we don't know where they

started? Discovering who you are and where you are purposed to be involves understanding where you came from and what those before you had to endure. Whether it is a burden or a blessing, it is a form of our inheritance. Whether we judge it to be good or bad, for many, our inheritance was one of survival. As you move through life, it is key to know all that you are carrying and whether you need to continue to carry it. Some gifts are meant to be carried on, but some must be laid down for us to navigate effectively. You may have heard the cliché that in death you can't take it with you, but so it is in life — not everything ought to be taken with us. The wounds of the past need to be exposed to be treated and healed. We may be walking with sores on our feet, untreated. They can worsen, slow us, and cause us to stumble. To enter purpose, you must understand the sources of pain.

As I continued my journey I reflected on these thoughts, knowing that each mile brought me closer to new beginnings and opportunities. The road ahead was not just a physical path but a metaphor for the inner journey I was undertaking: a journey of healing, discovery, and purpose. With each stop, I would uncover more about myself, my past, and the potential for my future.

This road trip was the beginning of a new chapter, one that would challenge me to confront my past, embrace the present, and look forward to the future with hope and determination. Little did I know that the landscapes I would traverse would not only shape my external journey but also my internal transformation.

Family Pattern to Unfold

Learned patterns from our past are key to understanding our habits today. Coping and survival methods help us understand the ways in which they have served us up to a point, but they may no longer serve in the same ways in the next phase of our life. Many of these patterns are passed down through generations. We repeat and respond to what we most often are exposed to. These habits can even become a family's culture but the next generation may be unaware of the benefits, reason, and their limitations. Family patterns, especially those ingrained from our family of origin, shape our sense of self and resilience in profound ways. Exploring these influences can offer valuable insight into our emotional responses, coping mechanisms and overall adaptability in the face of adversity. Consider these questions to reflect on your family patterns and their impact on your resilience:

1. *What messages about strength and vulnerability did you receive from your family growing up?*

2. *How did your family handle adversity, and how has that shaped your approach to challenges?*

3. *Were emotions openly expressed in your family, or were they suppressed? How has this influenced your ability to process emotions?*

4. *What role did you play in your family (e.g., caretaker, peacemaker, rebel), and how does that role still influence your interactions today?*

5. *How did your family view failure and success, and how has that impacted your self-worth and motivation?*

6. *Were resilience and perseverance encouraged in your family,*

or were setbacks seen as defeat?

7. *What generational patterns or cycles exist in your family, and how have they shaped your mindset and behaviors?*

8. *How do your current beliefs about relationships, trust, and support reflect the family environment you grew up in?*

9. *What positive strengths have you inherited from your family that contribute to your resilience today?*

10. *What aspects of your family patterns do you want to keep, and what do you need to unlearn in order to foster greater resilience and growth?*

NOTES

The next travel segment took me to Denver, Colorado, a city well-known for its high elevation and breathtaking mountain ranges. On the other hand, the first drive throughout the rest of Kansas's vast territory offered a striking contrast: an apparently never-ending flatland that extended to the horizons on both sides. As I battled the monotony of the terrain, I made the decision to make the drive more enjoyable.

I put the convertible top down and let the wind tickle my senses while turning up the volume on my music. This small deed turned the ordinary into a fun adventure. There was a long road ahead, and I could have driven on cruise control for hours on end without thinking twice. In retrospect, this part of the trip seems unremarkable, but from a different angle, it was a time of ease — a stretch I could take it easy on.

It was clear to see the surroundings develop in all directions; there were no sudden ups and downs. It was a clear, uninterrupted route, so I could unwind and almost forget about the typical distractions. During that period, the path's simplicity brought me comfort. The song remained like an echo in the wind, floating away over my shoulders as my thoughts drifted to possibilities. I imaged in life we long for times like this, when there is seemingly no obstruction, and we are still moving ahead. Nonetheless, it can be times like this where it is difficult to enjoy the moment and even appreciate the peace of clarity. Some of us might even have the need for more drama, stimulation or trauma. I can almost hear the child-like voice asking, "Are we there yet?" from the shear boredom of the flat land. It is important that we also master the moments that lack constant stimulation. Truthfully, it's not as though there is nothing to enjoy in those moments, we just tend to ignore them because they don't stimulate our senses the same.

Are you able to endure the uneventful? I longed for peace and to be undisturbed. To be on true cruise control. To be moving in life without having to stress or overthink and plan my next move. It was also too surreal to find comfort. I wanted to find stillness of mind and tune into to more subtle things in life, but my senses were heightened. The landscape felt like a treadmill screen whooshing by, there were many things to take in, but now in a different way.

The warmth of the air brushed over my arms. I could feel my grasp of the steering wheel light in my hands. The smell of the air was full and clean filtered through the green and browning earth. The lines of the highway were darting past me in a rhythm of progress and persistence. I was on my way to a new place and new chapter of possibilities.

The scenes set my mind to a truer transition period. I was in the shift from the past to a new future. I was in the moment to just be and let the earth carry me under the power of my engine.

As I finally embraced the tranquility of the scene and appreciated its steadfastness, I couldn't help but notice the gradual shift in the sky before me, as it began to be painted with a somber shade of gray. With gratitude guiding my perspective, I welcomed this change as another facet of nature's beauty to behold. As I continued driving towards it, it became evident that this gray veil wasn't simply a fleeting addition to the landscape; it was encroaching from all directions: west, south, and north. Having grown up in Indiana, I recognized this as the tell-tale sign of an impending storm. In the Midwest, such unpredictable weather occurrences were par for the course. Yet, there was an unmistakable weightiness to the atmosphere, a sense of foreboding that set this apart from the usual.

Pulling over, I swiftly secured the hardtop convertible, the mechanism moving it in felt like slow motion against the heavy backdrop of approach storm. With the top locked in place, I surveyed the western sky, only to be met with a sight both awe-inspiring and ominous — a colossal cloud looming, its mass stretching across the horizon like a scene from a sci-fi thriller. This was no ordinary storm; it was a spectacle of nature's fury, a flatland tempest brewing with an unsettling intensity.

The realization sent a shiver down my spine. Facing the possibility of encountering a tornado in the remote expanse of nowhere was a daunting prospect. Turning to the local AM station for guidance, the urgency in the broadcast matched the intensity of the pelting rain that now assaulted my precious car like shards of shattered glass. I was sure my car would be riddled with bullet-like dents. As my car trembled, buffeted by the force of the storm, I sought refuge under a bridge, joining the few other cars huddled there for shelter.

Beneath the bridge, the wind howled, and the hail lashed out in fierce bursts, testing the limits of our makeshift sanctuary. All we could do was wait, each impact of the hailstones against my car's exterior heightening the tension, each moment stretching into an eternity of uncertainty. As the storm gradually relented and the first glimmers of light pierced through the dissipating clouds, I looked at the glazed eyes of the drivers next to me. A collective sigh of relief echoed off of our windows.

Emerging cautiously from beneath the bridge, I marveled at the scene before me. Despite the ferocity of the storm, my car stood unscathed, a testament to its resilience in the face of nature's fury. With a sense of gratitude and awe mingling within me, I resumed my journey towards Silverthorne, Colorado, now acutely aware of the fragility of our existence in the face of such elemental forces. As I drove on, the radio's reassurance that the worst was over provided some measure of comfort, but the memory of the storm lingered; a reminder of nature's unfathomable power and our humble place within it.

Reflection after a Storm

Now, consider the unexpected storms you encounter on your life journey. It may or may not include a geographical change. It may be relational, financial or physical in nature. Whenever we are in the process of making a change, we are likely to hit unexpected threats of adversity. Understanding our initial emotional reactions to perceived danger can help us better cultivate our thoughts and our plans to respond; creating internal safe havens to reassure ourselves so we can move forward with intention and awareness. Here are some questions to help you shape a more resilient response to adversity:

1. *What is a situation wherein you initially perceived things as tranquil only to be confronted by an unexpected challenge?*

2. *How did you cope with the sudden shift in circumstances?*

3. *What things did you do to protect yourself from threat?*

4. *How did the situation impact your moving forward following the unexpected adversity?*

5. *How did that experience shape your self-concept when dealing with uncertainty?*

6. *What adverse impact did the situation have on your sense of safety?*

7. *How have past challenges influenced the way you prepare for potential future obstacles?*

8. *What strategies do you use to regain a sense of stability after a disruption?*

9. *How do you differentiate between real and perceived threats when facing uncertainty?*

10. *What role does self-compassion play in your ability to recover from adversity?*

NOTES

A Higher Place

Making my way to the next destination, I sought solace in the picturesque town of Silverthorne, Colorado, perched at an impressive elevation of approximately nine thousand feet above sea level. The breathtaking alpine vistas stretched before me, with majestic peaks crowned in pristine white snow during summer months. From the tumultuous uncertainty of the storm to the serene heights of the atmosphere, I found myself marveling at the tranquility that surrounded me.

After enduring over eight hours of focused driving, I yearned for respite, and Silverthorne promised the perfect sanctuary for the night, a temporary refuge before continuing my journey the next day.

As I arrived, I was greeted by a charming blend of rustic charm and modern convenience. The hotel accommodations, nestled amidst a backdrop of ski lodges, exuded a cozy cabin ambiance that instantly put me at ease. Despite having made no prior reservations, the convenience of modern technology allowed me to secure a room with ease, booking via my mobile phone as I entered the town.

Stepping out into the mountain village, I felt as though I had been transported back in time, the quaint charm of Silverthorne casting a nostalgic spell. I enjoyed a delicious meal at a local café, where I watched in awe as the sun descended behind the mountains, painting the sky in hues of blazing magenta, a breathtaking spectacle that seemed to momentarily suspend time itself.

The following morning, I greeted the dawn with eager anticipation, determined not to miss the spectacular sight of the sun's resurrection over the majestic mountains. Every sensation felt heightened, as if the world around me had been infused with a sense of newness and possibility. The air was crisp and invigorating, a refreshing embrace after the darkness of night.

Eager to immerse myself fully in the rejuvenating energy of the morning, I laced up my gym shoes and embarked on an early morning jog, arms outstretched to welcome the warming rays of the sun. With a confident stride, I set off towards a nearby hill, determined to make the most of the morning sun.

Yet, as I found my rhythm and pushed myself uphill, I soon felt my breath grow labored and my heart pounding furiously within the confines of my chest. Despite my initial enthusiasm, I found myself gasping for air, my body struggling to cope with the thinness of the high-altitude. Bent over, hands on knees, I felt as winded as a boxer after nine grueling rounds, despite having only run a mere three blocks. It was a humbling reminder of the power of nature's elements, and the importance of respecting their influence on our physical capabilities.

The encounter with the unforgiving altitude served as a poignant reminder of our limitations, even amidst the breathtaking beauty. Despite being surrounded by picturesque landscapes, I was unprepared for the thin air. It was a humbling realization, highlighting the importance of understanding and adapting to our surroundings, no matter how idyllic they may seem at first glance. It was a lesson in humility, a reminder that even in the most captivating environments, there are limitations to our endurance. There is a period that requires training and adaptation to any new environment, especially at a higher level.

As I made my way back to the hotel room, each step weighted with introspection, I resolved to approach the next leg of my journey with patience and awareness. It was a lesson learned through hardship, a testament to the importance of embracing my vulnerabilities and to pace myself. I realized though I had set out to conquer the day with my morning jog, I simply was not prepared internally. I had to be okay with that. To be fit for this altitude, I would have had to take much more time practicing.

It is not uncommon for us to encounter events or places in our life where we find our ability is limited. Sometimes we may even think we are ready to take on something more, but our readiness is tested as we enter a new space. Reflecting on experiences of struggling to adapt to the unseen changes in the atmosphere I experienced, I ask you to consider your own experiences and answer these questions:

1. *Have you ever found yourself in a situation where the surroundings contradicted the challenges hidden within? How did you navigate the unexpected difficulties you encountered?*

2. *Have you ever felt like you were an imposter when you entered a new environment? What did you become aware of about yourself and how did you adapt?*

3. *Can you recall a time when you felt unprepared for the demands of a new environment, job or partnership? How did you cope with the unfamiliarity and adversity?*

4. *In what ways have you changed in the face of unexpected challenges or limitations?*

5. *Have you ever experienced a moment of vulnerability that led to personal growth or self-awareness? What lessons did*

you glean from that experience?

6. *How do you prepare yourself to adapt to new environments or circumstances? What techniques do you employ to cultivate resilience in the face of uncertainty?*

NOTES

Gaining Perspective

After catching my breath, I gathered my belongings, bracing myself for another arduous ten-hour stretch on the road. Destination: Las Vegas. It was midweek now, Wednesday, and my intention was to grant myself a single day of respite in the vibrant city of lights before embarking on the final leg of my journey to California. My new job awaited, start date of Tuesday, July 5th, a date etched with significance — the anniversary of the kidney donation to my chosen dad that forever altered the course of my life.

The transplant had been christened by the hospital as "A second chance at life," a profound truth that resonated within me. Memories of the trials and triumphs of that miraculous procedure flooded my mind, reminding me of the journey I had undertaken and the healing it had bestowed. I found it mystical that these dates happened to align. Now, July 5th would not only mark the commencement of a new job but also symbolize a personal odyssey of self-discovery and renewal. My plan was to bring my dad out to California as well to allow him to continue to enjoy his second chance at life. I wanted to honor his journey and glean from his guidance in this next phase.

Living in California held a profound significance beyond just a new job opportunity; it was a chance to delve into my own family history. My biological father had woven the tapestry of his life in the Bay Area, where he crossed paths with my mother and where my late sister, Amber, was conceived. Her dream of living in California seemed to linger in the air, a whisper of companionship on my journey.

Growing up without our father's presence, my sister and I harbored a curiosity about his life and his path. I pondered the places he had frequented, the experiences that had shaped him, and how this landscape might influence my own journey. In many ways, this transition to California was not just about forging ahead; it was about connecting with my roots, understanding the lineage that had led me to this moment.

Dr. Maya Angelou's timeless adage echoed in my mind: "You can't know where you are going until you know where you have been." California wasn't just a destination; it was a bridge between past and future, a landscape teeming with stories waiting to be unearthed. As I embarked on this new chapter I carried with me the echoes of my family's legacy, ready to weave my own narrative amidst the storied hills and valleys of the Golden State.

Contemplating these thoughts, I traversed the winding roads from Colorado through Utah to Nevada, the towering cliffs and cascading waterfalls serving as silent witnesses to the passage of time. They carried the weight of their past, each crevice and rivulet a testament to the journey that had shaped them. In their presence, I found solace and perspective, acknowledging the interconnectedness of past, present, and future.

Leaving behind the familiar comforts of home, I embraced the uncertainty of the road ahead, recognizing my past was not something to be discarded but rather revered. It was the foundation upon which my future would be built, a repository of invaluable lessons and experiences meant to guide me forward. Though I could not rewrite history or dwell in regret, I bore the responsibility of honoring its significance, embracing the richness of its meaning as I embarked on this new chapter of my life's journey.

Before we go further on the journey, take a moment to delve into these introspective questions here. Deeper understanding of ourselves and finding greater direction necessitates a curious exploration of our own journey. These questions are crafted to guide you in reflecting on your past experiences, unraveling the threads that have woven the tapestry of your life thus far, and gaining insight into the path you want to be traveling.

Let's review the significance of your journey by answering these questions.

1. *What pivotal moments or experiences from your past continue to shape your beliefs, values, and decisions in the present?*

2. *How have past challenges and setbacks influenced your resilience and ability to overcome obstacles in your life?*

3. *What recurring patterns or themes do you notice in your past experiences, and how might they be guiding you towards a certain path or direction?*

4. *In what ways have past relationships, both family and personal, impacted your sense of identity and self-worth?*

5. *Reflecting on past accomplishments and achievements, what strengths and talents have you cultivated that can serve as resources for navigating future opportunities and challenges?*

6. *How do moments of transition in your life — whether expected or unexpected — serve as opportunities for personal growth and transformation?*

7. *What aspects of your past do you struggle to embrace, and*

how might reframing them help you move forward with greater peace and acceptance?

8. *In what ways do your personal and family history influence the goals and dreams you pursue today?*

9. *If you were to view your journey as a story, what themes or lessons emerge, and how do they shape the next chapter you wish to write?*

NOTES

Warning Signals

As the sun reached its peak, I found myself traversing the scorching landscape of northern Nevada, the relentless heat of triple-digit temperatures pressing against the car's exterior. Inside, the convertible top remained firmly sealed, the air conditioner struggling to provide respite from the oppressive heat. Amidst this discomfort, a sudden flash of the engine light shattered the monotony of the journey, casting an unwelcome glow on the dashboard.

My initial reaction was one of frustration, an exasperated sigh escaping my lips as I grappled with the implications of the warning light. Though the car showed no signs of distress, I couldn't afford to dismiss the alert, not with the vast expanse of the Nevada desert stretching ahead of me. With a sense of urgency gnawing at my insides, I made the decision to pull off at the nearest gas station, hoping that a simple restart would banish the ominous glow.

As I turned off the ignition and offered a silent prayer to the automotive gods, I braced myself for the outcome. Yet, despite my hopeful anticipation, the light remained stubbornly illuminated, a persistent reminder of the potential peril lurking beneath the hood. With a resigned acceptance, I acknowledged the need to seek professional assistance before pressing on, lest I risk exacerbating the issue further.

Mindful of the specialized needs of my BMW, I searched to find a reputable repair shop equipped to handle the intricacies of the engineering. Concerns about exorbitant costs and the reliability of the mechanics weighed heavily on my mind as I scoured the area for viable options. Finally, a glimmer of hope emerged as I stumbled upon a qualified mechanic in a nearby town, the extra stars on their reviews helped to soothe my frayed nerves.

With a mixture of relief and gratitude, I contacted the shop, explaining my predicament and my imminent arrival. Fortunately, they agreed to accommodate me without the need for an appointment, a stroke of fate that I couldn't help but marvel at in hindsight. Reflecting on this fortuitous turn of events, I realized the importance of preparation and resourcefulness in navigating unexpected detours.

Indeed, the flashing warning light on the car's dashboard served as a poignant metaphor for life's journey — an internal indicator urging us to pause, reassess and perhaps even change course when necessary. Just as we heed the signs and alerts along the road, so too must we learn to recognize and respond to the signals that life presents us with.

In hindsight, it's easy to see how ignoring those warning lights could lead to greater problems down the road. However, true wisdom lies in having the foresight to anticipate potential obstacles and taking proactive measures to address them. Much like navigating the twists and turns of the open road, navigating life requires a keen awareness of our surroundings and a willingness to seek expert guidance when needed.

Thankfully, the issue was nothing more than a sensor that needed replacement. Once it was fixed, I could travel on without the nagging concern of what might have been wrong if I had ignored that warning sign. It certainly could have been worse, potentially leading to a more serious problem had I dismissed the warning and continued driving. I envisioned myself stranded in the desert, dehydrated, with tumbleweeds bouncing by and no cellphone service — not an image I wanted to experience.

Grateful to the technician at the repair shop, I was back on the road in under two hours. While I lost some time, I appreciated the greater amount of time and potential cost I might have faced had I tried to press on without addressing the issue. I was eager to reach my respite in Las Vegas, but the experience underscored the necessity of patience and the importance of attending to issues promptly.

Embracing the delay with a sense of purpose, I realized that sometimes, more work is needed before pressing ahead. Surrendering my own timeline and recognizing the priority of necessary repairs was a valuable lesson. This experience taught me to appreciate the importance of patience and the foresight to prevent minor issues from escalating into major problems.

So, the next time you encounter a flashing warning light on your metaphorical dashboard, don't hesitate to pull over and ask for help. Trust in the wisdom of seeking expert assistance and guidance, for it is often the surest path to avoiding further damage and ensuring a smooth journey ahead. These questions are for you to reflect on attending to your personal warning signals.

1. *Can you recall a time when you ignored an important alert or warning in your life, only to later face consequences as a result?*

2. *What internal or external signals do you typically overlook or dismiss in your daily life, and what impact have they had on your decision-making process?*

3. *Reflecting on past experiences, what patterns or tendencies have you noticed in your response to alerts or warnings? How have these patterns influenced the outcomes of your actions?*

4. Is there a specific built-in indicator or gut feeling that serves as your personal alarm system, alerting you to potential problems or dangers? How do you typically respond when this indicator is activated?

5. In hindsight, what lessons have you learned from instances where you failed to heed warnings or alerts in your life?

6. How can you apply these insights to cultivate a greater sense of awareness and responsiveness moving forward?

NOTES

Respite and Rejuvenate

As I made my way toward Las Vegas, the journey transformed into a breathtaking spectacle. The sunset breaking over the red cliffs painted a stunning display of natural artistry around every bend in the road. At that moment, I realized how rare and precious these sights were. The air was still warm, making the experience even more enjoyable. Eagerly, I sought out each new view, as if the landscape were a series of sculptures showcased on nature's grand stage. My eyes darted to capture the next masterpiece before the sun dipped below the horizon, its final act lighting up the sky in a brilliant display.

Though I was behind my planned schedule, I felt a deep sense of gratitude. The delay had allowed me to witness this extraordinary evening show put on by nature. As the hours passed, I drew closer to my destination: Las Vegas. A new kind of illumination began to emerge, lighting up the sky from the ground up. From a distance, the vibrant glow of the city penetrated the shadowy night, and the welcoming brightness of roadside signs signaled my approach. It felt like a genuine greeting after the long hours on the road.

Driving onto the Strip, it was as if I were entering a movie scene. With the top down on my convertible, I cruised under the canopy of dazzling lights, soaking in the moment. I maintained a cruise, savoring the flashes and the vibrant scenery around me. It felt like I was on my own stage, the city lights dancing around me, marking a triumphant transition in my journey thus far.

I navigated to the end of the Strip, where the golden bronze hotel rose like a trophy behind the other casinos. Despite the city's vibrant energy, I was ready for some much-needed rest. I had planned a two-night stay, giving myself time to recharge.

As I checked into the luxury hotel, I knew this would be the pinnacle of my trip. The atmosphere immediately bestowed a sense of VIP swag upon me, and just walking through the opulent lobby made me feel successful. I took a moment to soak it all in before making my way to my suite. Entering the room, I felt a wave of relief and contentment wash over me. It was time to rest and conclude the day's journey, knowing that I had reached a place of comfort and luxury where I could truly unwind.

The next morning, I woke up with a deep sense of appreciation. I was now halfway to my destination and had a full day ahead to rest and rejuvenate. I wasn't in Las Vegas for the customary experience; after hundreds of miles on the road, my goal was to get a great workout in and take full advantage of the hotel's amenities and spa. I spent the day indulging in a soothing massage and soaking up the views by the pool. This might be the only day of vacation I would have for a while, as I was about to start my new job as COO at a psychiatric hospital.

This day of relaxation was a rare and cherished opportunity to reset before diving into the demanding responsibilities awaiting me. As I enjoyed the luxurious surroundings, I felt a renewed sense of energy and purpose, ready to take on the challenges ahead.

As you journey through your own life's path, it's essential to recognize the moments when you need to pause and recharge. Reflecting on your personal needs and strategies for self-care can lead to a more balanced and purposeful life.

Take a moment to consider these questions. Reflect deeply and write down your answers, allowing yourself to explore how you can better integrate rest and recovery into your routine.

1. How do you recognize the signs in yourself that it's time to take a break and seek rest?

2. What activities or environments help you feel truly recharged and rejuvenated?

3. When was the last time you dedicated a day solely to rest and self-care and how did it affect your wellbeing?

4. How do you balance the demands of your responsibilities with the need for self-care and mental rejuvenation?

5. In what ways does taking time to rest and recharge contribute to your sense of purpose and effectiveness in your work or personal life?

By thoughtfully considering these questions and writing down your responses, you'll gain valuable insights into how you can better care for yourself and sustain your energy and purpose on your journey.

It may not have been the typical stay of all-night partying in Las Vegas, as one might expect, but my intentions were geared towards restoration, not indulgence. Early the next morning, I set off to continue the final leg of my journey. The remaining eight-hour road trip was to San Jose, California. My small car was packed full of my essentials, enough to last for the week until I could ship everything else from Indiana to California and fly my dad out, too.

The gap between where I was and what I wanted felt closer now on this final leg. Though there were many unknowns ahead,

I was excited to explore and discover this new chapter. The hurt of losing my sister to suicide still stung in my chest. These were moments I wanted to share with her and bring her along. She would have been proud and excited to come along. I felt the frustration of her life being cut short, knowing there was so much more she could have done. Even though I was driving further from those painful memories, the spirit of her hope remained with me. Her death and remaining call now rolled into my own. The waves of grief would still catch me from time to time, but they were now pushing me toward greater shores.

I reflected on the many milestones growing up with my sister Amber. She was two years older than I and often took on the role of babysitter, more often than she should have, at an early age. While our mother was at work, Amber was the person I leaned on. I think I overestimated her ability to look out for me and underestimated the amount of pressure she felt when we were alone. For instance, there was the time we ate too many Flintstone vitamins and got sick, and the time we snacked on dry cat food. One of the more vivid memories was when I had the bright idea to put a fork in the light socket. The resulting spark sent spinning circles of light across the floor, and the tips of my fingers were seared from the blast, leaving me bawling in tears as I sought something to remedy the pain. So yes, my sister wasn't great at babysitting me. Sometimes I wondered if it was her secret plan to get rid of me, or maybe she simply wasn't thrilled about having to look after me. Either way, her intentions were a mystery to me back then, and the thought of it now made me laugh. We were just children, competing for limited time and attention.

Ultimately, we were put under the supervision of various neighborhood babysitters when our mom was away at work. Unfortunately this arrangement was less than ideal as we were both exposed to more untoward things than we should have experienced as children. Reflecting on it all made my heart ache.

Whether she liked it or not, by birth order, my sister went first on most things. She was the trailblazer. I remember, as a kid, looking to her as a barometer: if she struggled with something, it must be hard. If she had a tough time with math in school, I approached it with caution. If she could climb the jungle gym at the playground, then I could surely do it too. She was first in school, first in relationships, and first to leave home. In early adolescence, she gave me insights on what girls liked, and I would try to impress her friends with my immature charisma and dance moves.

I admired the courage this must have taken, especially since we didn't have a visual anchor. Our father was absent for much of our young lives. The last time I saw him, I was eight years old, so my sister must have been about ten. We had no idea we would never see him again for the rest of our lives. He was a looming shadow that never entered the room again. Neither of us had insights into the dynamics that contributed to the divide between him and our mother. Maybe it was something I could discover. My sister and I were both the first children born in our mother's family, so we didn't have the guidance of older cousins either. We were far removed from our father's side of the family, and though we were kin by blood, there was no active influence from that branch of our tree.

Amber and our mother were often in conflict, and I was frequently the mediator. Amid the turmoil, my sister ultimately moved out of the home by the time she was sixteen to be with an older boyfriend, to whom she was emancipated. She went to a different school by the time I entered high school. Following her lead, I moved out at fifteen to attend a residential school at a nearby university. Fortunately, my academic performance was good enough to afford me other opportunities. I was more motivated to leave as a teenager to find my own way rather than purely to achieve. I noticed many other kids there had substantial support and presence from their parents. Without the oversight of my sister or her example to follow, I started to blaze my own trail. Regardless of the situation, thankfully, it put me on a path of using education to journey towards something better.

The last time I saw my sister alive was on Christmas Day in 2013. When I entered the front door, she gave me the biggest embrace — as if I were her last friend. She apologized and said she was sorry for everything. At the time, it felt like she was apologizing for the prior few months, where her depression and irritability had set her temper ablaze with most everyone. I told her there was no need and that I loved her. She remembered that I was always on her side. Maybe she was also apologizing for all the things she did and didn't do when we were kids. The answer to that was unclear but I accepted it.

Sitting in the small, dark living room of someone else's home, we reminisced about all the silly antics we did as kids, including the mishaps of her babysitting. Though our reunion cheered the room, it didn't have the aura of Christmas that one would come to expect. Amber slept in a makeshift room in the back of the garage. It was hard to see her in this place now, given she had worked so hard to change her course in life. We had spent much time imagining creating a better life outside of our apartment complex. Her daughter, then thirteen years old, was there too, grateful just to be near her mom. Our mother was also visiting that evening. The television was on with a holiday film flickering in the dark room.

My sister, at thirty-six years old, had managed to establish a better life for her daughter than where we were at that same age. This would be the last time we would be in the same place together. None of us knew that my sister had only six more days on earth. Maybe that was what her apology was truly about. Forgiving her for the assault on her own life was difficult but necessary to find healing.

When anyone dies who we love, the cause of their death often becomes the enemy. Whether it is by an ailment such as cancer, heart disease or stroke, or from another tragic event such as a drunk driver, gun violence, an accident or a murder, we naturally seek a target for our anger and grief. We righteously fight against cancer, heart disease, AIDS, diabetes and gun violence after a loved one dies, channeling our pain into action.

However, with suicide, the grief is more complicated. You might find yourself angry at the person who died, because they themselves ended their life. You may also blame yourself, feeling that you didn't love them enough to help them stay. In our grief, we often search for a source of the pain. If you believe that suicide is a choice, you can become infuriated with the idea that the person chose death over life. This is a limited and overly-simplistic rationale, however. Suicide involves many cumulative factors that are difficult to unravel. The unanswered *whys* in death often lead to empty rooms of confusion and sorrow.

When you begin to empathize with the emotional pain that someone might have been feeling, you start to understand their struggle with a new perspective. You see the dark cloud and the shadows blocking their hope. Yet, even as you grasp the depth of their despair, you recognize that there was a way out, though they could not see it. This understanding fuels a greater search to equip oneself for the battle against this insidious enemy in the shadows.

So, here I found myself on a greater journey of discovery and healing. I sought out more answers beyond what happened to my sister. I knew it was a problem for many more people and their families. As director of a crisis program, I saw often the frustration of getting access to quality care. With this new job opportunity, I hoped I would be better positioned to make a difference in health-care delivery and systems of treatment. I believed my sister had fallen through cracks of the system. I wanted to find ways to fix these issues and leadership was the place. Above all, I wanted to help others fight the stigma of mental health and addiction, and to provide quality care.

Exploring Your Tree

The other part of this journey was discovering family. The death of my sister left a chasm in the family tree, yet there were other family members on my father's side with whom we had minimal contact. I imagined that connecting with them might help me resolve my grief further. Maybe knowing them more would help fill the void.

I had two half-sisters in California, Angela and DeDe, and a half-brother, Mikel, who lived in Seattle. They had more insights about our father and his story, along with unique experiences with their mother, who was living in California. They were children when my father, Henry C. Rollins, traveled to Rome, Italy in the 1960s as a fellow at the American Academy of Fine Arts. In fact, the youngest, DeDe, was born in Italy.

Mikel, the eldest, was a prodigy musician who could play practically any instrument, from the saxophone to the guitar, on demand. He had a calm, laid-back energy and was seemingly unbothered by most things, always preferring to avoid conflict. His deep, raspy voice vibrated over the phone when we talked, an echo of mine and our father's. Talking with him was a familiar tune. "Hey! Hey! What up, Bro?" he would chime on the rare occasions we talked.

Angela was the quintessential middle child, a mediator among the family, both present and past. She was ever on a quest for justice and truth, enchanted by all things in the universe. She lived simply and in isolation, valuing all things sacred: the flowers, the trees, the wild animals — anything that took a breath or gave breath was of value in her world. She was an avid Buddhist and faithfully attended AA meetings. She had once visited my sister Amber and me when we were young teenagers. I had drawn a large portrait of her that she kept. She lived near her mother in California and was the keeper of our father's ashes. Before Amber ended her life, she had coordinated and paid for the cremation herself, shipping the ashes to Angela. Amber died before we were able to do anything with our father's ashes together.

With DeDe, the youngest, I was much less familiar. She lived solo and, like Angela, had no children. Though I had never talked to her in my adult life, I had photographs of her and my sister playing in the park when we were small children. It looked like I was about three years old and my sister was five. I wore little cowboy boots and a t-shirt with a baseball on the front, while my sister was in a red and white dress like a doll. There was one photo of me sitting on her lap atop a sculpted turtle — her with an afro, wearing Jordache jeans. Apparently, at the age of eighteen, she moved from Seattle, Washington, with my sister, my mom, and our father to live in Indiana where my mother was from. The Midwest was apparently not the place for her so she quickly returned west. However, I didn't understand why I hadn't heard from her much growing up.

Mikel had two lovely daughters. One daughter, Erika, lived out east, a Howard University graduate, married with two young boys, and got her doctorate degree in Educational Policy. She was a stable soul, and we had connected, establishing a healthy bond. Sadly, she never had the opportunity to meet my sister. Mikel's younger daughter, Carmen, was always on the move. I had seen her once when she was very young, years ago, when I was visiting Seattle. We had talked a few times before, and from what I knew, she was living in Cabo. I was eager to connect with all of them and learn more. At the age of 38 I was realizing how little I knew about that side of my family.

Our father, Henry, or sometimes referred to as Hank, had been found deceased in February 2013 in the back of a home previously owned by his aunt in Oregon who had died and left the home vacant. According to the coroner's report, his body was found emaciated in that back studio of the house, his fingers and toes gnawed by rodents. The cause of death was recorded as hypothermia. It felt like such a loathsome mysterious exit from this world. Amber was devastated by the findings. She had been reaching for some meaningful connection before she ended her life. She had gone so far as to have our father cremated, but she never lived long enough to see his ashes or burial. In her grief, my sister seemed to have lost touch with herself more after our father died. Overtaken by the darkness of depression she felt emaciated in her soul.

There seemed to be so much division within our family. We were siblings, all disjointed, and Amber was gone. So many gifts and so much beauty yet broken apart like a fallen stained-glass window. There were pieces missing. Processing the meaning of all this weighed heavily on my heart as I drove.

I had come so far on this journey, but things had not transpired as I had imagined. Goals in family, love and work seemed to keep falling just out of reach, like mirages on the desert floor. The road ahead was uncertain, but maybe this next chapter held the key to healing and reconnection. I was not out of hope, so I traveled on, pushing my foot harder on the gas pedal, determined to find answers and solace.

To not become disheartened, I decided to call my niece, Carmen. She was far enough removed from all the turmoil to offer a fresh perspective. "Hello!" she said, excitement in her voice. Her tone was light and cheery. I remembered seeing pictures of her when she was a child, her eyes bright and her head-full of rose-colored curls. Her energy matched her pictures. She felt like a warm wind circling the sun: refreshing and hopeful.

I told her about my travels, and she was intrigued. "How far have you come? How far do you have to go?" she inquired. She was enthusiastic about the possibility of meeting. She was also fluent in Spanish, so we practiced vocabulary and phrases as I drove. We laughed as I stumbled over phrases. We talked about her career aspirations; she told me about her plans to be a flight attendant; a job that seemed to match her free-flowing spirit.

I told her I would plan to visit her once I got settled in California, or if she was ever visiting her grandmother, I would come to see her. It was a comforting call and something to look forward to. I felt an immediate bond with her.

This new connection gave me a sense of hope and something

to anchor myself to as I continued my journey. The open road ahead felt a little less daunting, knowing I had family waiting to welcome me into this new chapter of my life.

One's family, whether born into or adopted, plays a significant role in how we interact with the world. Our sense of belonging, attachment, acceptance and safety are influenced by family dynamics. There are some elements in family systems that maybe unable to shift; but having awareness of them enables us to adapt with more intention. Regardless of status, these important relationships can influence how we move through the world and find healthy connections with others. The questions here are designed to help you to gain insights. Please take time to reflect on your family experiences, however it is designed. I have added additional prompts as a guide since family dynamics can be particularly challenging.

1. *How do your family relationships influence your identity and sense of belonging?*

    How do your connections with different family members contribute to your understanding of who you are?

2. *In what ways have family dynamics shaped your perceptions of love and conflict?*

    Consider specific experiences within your family that have defined your views on relationships and how you handle disagreements.

3. *What pieces of your family history do you feel are missing, and how might discovering them impact your understand-*

ing of yourself? Are there any gaps in your knowledge about your family's past? How might filling those gaps influence your personal narrative?

4. How do you cope with feelings of disconnection or fragmentation within your family? What strategies do you use for dealing with distance or conflict among family members and how do these strategies affect your emotional wellbeing?

5. What steps can you take to strengthen your connections with family members with whom you feel distant?

Consider actions you can take to bridge gaps and build stronger relationships with family members, and how doing so might enrich your sense of self.

The Final Stretch

Breaking through the daunting desert landscape, I made my way through Southern California's Mojave Desert. It was nothing like the heavy, lush corn and soybean fields back in Indiana. The air was dry and crisp. The landscape was prickled with cacti, coarse shrubs, and hot stony ground. The sky felt longer here. The horizon line looked like the center of a turning page in a book where the smooth blue sky met the textured ground. Even though this was a new chapter in my story, I could sense I was taking the pain of what happened with me, as much as I wanted to erase it from my pages.

In this passage, it felt as though many stories were etched into the rocky, dry land. The coarse ground kept a record of troubles, blown over by the sandy winds, but the fine print remained there. I pulled over on the side of the road to gaze at the scene and release my own story here. The air was whooshing with the sounds of passing cars, and a raven's call went out with no echoing back. The wind blew over my skin like a surge of electricity. My breath heated the back of my throat, swelling my chest with the air. I wanted to release and drop my sorrows here and let them burn away like a sacrifice in the sun. As I stared into the center page of the horizon, I wondered if my grief would dissipate, or if it would remain carved in my heart like the stories in this landscape.

This was a place of transition: the final stretch. This was the home of the Joshua Tree. The resilient yucca tree was the native symbol here, with its arm-like branches reaching for the sky. It served as a reminder that even in pain, desperation, and uncertainty, one should still reach up. I collected the warm air in a deep breath and poured into it my own pains and exhaled in exchange for greater hope. I knew the pain served a purpose and the salve was to keep going forward. The next page of the sky would carry me.

I was about four hours out now from my destination in San Jose. As I drove deeper into California, the landscape began to shift dramatically. The rugged rocky cliffs gradually gave way to rolling hills draped in a lush, green carpet. It felt as though the ground was covered by a cashmere blanket, soft and inviting. The familiar scent of rich soil and farmland filled the air, a stark contrast to the arid desert I had left behind. The scene gave me a sense of inner comfort. I knew there would be growth here. This place felt like fertile ground for new beginnings. The sun was plentiful, casting a warm glow over the expansive fields. I couldn't help but wonder how this land would shape and nurture me. Could it soothe my soul, or would it add more weight to my already heavy heart? I was driven by a desire to escape past hurts and filled with the hope of growing something new.

As I headed further north, the vastness of the landscape enveloped me. This wasn't the California of dense cityscapes and iconic palm trees I had idealized. Instead, I found myself immersed in the tranquil countryside. Trucks loaded with various goods from crops to livestock rumbled along the highways, a testament to the region's agricultural abundance. From the dry desert to this landscape of production, I was reminded of the of importance of our environment. I passed landscapes adorned with solar panels, glistening like glass mosaics under the sun, and fields dotted with giant wind turbines, their blades turning slowly against the clear sky. The air was thick with the industrious hum of energy production, from the solar farms to the wind farms. It was a symphony of progress and nature coexisting.

Traveling above seventy miles an hour, I witnessed the scenes on display while hearing the road zip and click under my tires. The urge is to move on or fail to produce. The pressure is to produce something outward as the symbol, the fruit of our efforts. I desired to make a difference in the lives of others; to serve and nourish others. It was one to way to make up for the death of my sister. Was my heart broken enough to be tilled? I wondered if I was too broken. I wondered if I could even make a difference in such vast landscape. I knew I could not become hardened like the desert landscape. Though the hardness looked strong, everything there seemed forced. It was scary to be open. My next phase, in Fremont, California, was to take on a higher leadership role. I questioned whether I could lead from a place of vulnerability or was more grit and firmness required. To be rigid felt like I would be disingenuous.

Driving with the top down, I relished the open air until a pungent smell hit me. Nearing a ranch, the heavy scent of cow dung forced me to retreat and close the top of my car. The smell stretched for miles: a raw reminder of the organic nature of this land. It was a sensory overload, but it also reminded me of the raw, unfiltered experiences that lay ahead. I was intrigued by so many changes in one state. Other places I had traveled the scenery seemed to repeat endlessly. Here, it was a matter of hours before the landscape would shift to a new scene. I found myself driving through steep hills as though I was riding the waves of the ocean but made of soil. The hillside swept up and down and I gripped the wheel and took the curves like a roller coaster ride. It was hard not to turn my head in awe of what would be around the next bend in the road. My heart beat harder in my chest with the anticipation.

As I approached San Jose, my thoughts drifted to what awaited me. Fortunately, the summer days were long, allowing me to witness the city's scenes before dusk. This city represented more than just a new location; it was a symbol of hope and renewal. I imagined walking through its streets, meeting new people, and finding a sense of belonging. The anticipation was palpable, mingled with a touch of apprehension. Would this place live up to my expectations? Would I live up to the expectations I set for myself? As much as I was focused on my career, I also pondered whether I would find love here. After a difficult breakup years ago, that was an adventure I was much more timid about.

My ex-girlfriend, May, had decided to give her love to another man just as I was planning to propose to strengthen our relationship. It was a great betrayal of my affections. In my attachment, I was blind to what was happening. She accepted his offer the day my sister ended her life. May did not know that as she was beginning to create the family with someone else which I had hoped for, I lost part of mine.

Now I hoped that if I could make time to meet people, I might feel more connected. In my heart, I wanted companionship, but I was afraid of being hurt again. The remedy for heartache was as complex as the health-care system, if not more so. The pursuit of a relationship was a journey that a navigation system could not guide me through. It was possible, though, that it lay somewhere up ahead. I liked the idea of that, yet the timing was unknown. I resolved to stay open to a relationship but remain guarded.

Arriving in San Jose, the first thing that struck me was the vibrant energy of the city. The air buzzed with activity, a stark contrast to the serene countryside I had just passed through. Winding highways overhead, tall buildings, and bright streets welcomed me, and I felt a mix of excitement and nervousness. I was certainly not in Kansas anymore; I was in the heart of Silicon Valley. Here, amidst the new sights and sounds, I hoped to carve out a new chapter in my life, one filled with growth, connection, and healing.

Exhausted from the drive and filled with visions of anticipation, I made my way to the room I had rented for the week. It was a small room on the top floor of a family's home. The home smelled of warmth and curry. I gathered a few of my bags just for the night and left my shoes near the front door as was customary. This would be my home for the first week in the Bay.

The first task of the new day was to look for an apartment. I had the weekend to explore, and with July 4th falling on a Monday that year, it gave me a bit more time. I was aware that navigating traffic at specific times of the day would be a critical part of my commute. I would be working at a psychiatric hospital in Fremont, located in the East Bay. Ideally, I needed to find an affordable apartment close to the hospital. In that area it meant traveling north in the morning and south in the evenings. Given the size of San Jose and all the technology companies there, most people were clamoring on the highways to work there in the morning. That narrowed my search to Fremont or south of it to avoid a hectic commute.

I started my search for a place from Fremont and went southwards. I searched for a two-bedroom place with accessibility to accommodate my dad when he moved to California. I was quickly stunned by the price difference. I knew they would be higher than back in Indiana, but they were three times the cost for the same square footage. It wasn't just the price that was an issue. The places I was seeing were sorely outdated. This was my first encounter with paying more and getting less. Apparently, included in the price was the ideal climate outdoors. Knowing I wouldn't be able to avoid the higher cost, I pursued at least finding a nicer place. Surprisingly, that led me further from the workplace to an upscale apartment complex in North San Jose. Thankfully, it had covered parking and an elevator for my dad to traverse without stairs. This seemed to fit the bill. But the cost was unavoidable. The high price made the six-figure salary I would be getting with my new job no more gain than what I was making back in Indiana. I tried not to dwell on the fact that after the cost of living here, it was a lateral move. The warm sun and bright views soothed my concerns. I was a short drive to the ocean, beaches and the enticing cities. I took the view that I was not in a place of scarcity but of opportunities.

With my apartment secured, I decided to take the remainder of the holiday weekend to explore the surrounding communities.

This was my new hometown, and I wanted to immerse myself in it and feel like I belonged. My goal was to see as many sights as I could and to take nothing for granted.

My first destination was the Oakland Museum, where a forty-foot steel sculpture called Anansi, created by my biological father, Henry Rollins, stood proudly. Anansi, a spider figure from West African folklore, was the son of Mother Earth and the Father Sky. As the King of Stories, Anansi used his wit to trick his enemies, passing down wisdom to generations on how to use intelligence and perseverance to overcome adversity. Anansi was an intercessor between the sky and the world.

The sculpture was prominently placed directly across from the main entrance, serving as a tribute to my father's artistry. The abstract piece stood atop a red cylinder base, towering as though it were climbing to reach over the four-story building up to the sky. Walking up next to it, I was awestruck by its scale and presence. The metallic sheen of the spider's legs caught the sunlight, casting intricate shadows on the ground.

Staring up at the sculpture, I felt a surge of determination. Like Anansi, I was about to embark on a journey full of challenges in this new state. I wondered if maybe my father had left this message for me. But Anansi was created before I was born, so it seemed unlikely. Yet here I was, receiving its message loud and clear. I could see in his work the attempt to unlock the stories that an artist needs to tell: an unspoken wisdom encapsulated in a symbol.

For me, it was a call to carry on this part of his journey somehow. The wisdom still needed to be unlocked with keys of creativity and persistence. The obstacles I would face seemed more surmountable as I stood in the shadow of Anansi, drawing strength from the legacy of both the sculpture and the stories it represented.

Oakland was full of intrigue and cultural energy. Each encounter, sight, and story intertwined, much like Anansi's web, reinforcing my belief that I was where I needed to be, part of this intricate plot. The Bay would be a place of discovery and exploration. I remembered that my sister Amber had once visited nearby; I had seen pictures of her in Jack London Square when she came to visit our other sisters years ago. I didn't know if she had ever encountered Anansi, but I felt her spirit nearby. Anansi served as a memorial for both my father and her now. There were mysteries to untangle in its web and new wisdoms to discover in its balanced design. These images filled me with hope, and I felt a sense of peace about what the future here would hold.

On the Fourth of July, I decided to cruise around the East Bay: from San Jose to Palo Alto to San Mateo to San Francisco and back to Mountain View to see the fireworks display. With the top down, I soaked in all I could as a preview of what was in store. The water in the bay lay to the east, while the landscape of suburbs, cityscapes and cypress trees stretched to my west. Since it was a holiday, there was less traffic than usual, giving me the freedom to drive at will. The air was warm and then cool, floating through the micro-climates. The Bay felt like a homemade stew with all kinds of ingredients, each stimulating the senses in a new way. Together, they created a harmonious balance: the cool air and warm sun, the pale blue sky and green trees, the crisp water breaking into stony gem shores and the old architecture complemented by new, modern shapes. The bridges tied the bay together like a platter. There was plenty to consume, and I knew I would not be able to indulge in it all at once.

I reflected on the events of three years prior, in July, when I donated a kidney to my pastor and chosen father, who had been a mentor to me since high school. The memory of that divine call, a miracle that replayed in my mind, was still vivid. When God speaks to you, you must be willing to receive and act in faith. I had learned that a willing heart precedes direction from God. Being in a place of surrendered uncertainty creates an opportunity for miracles to take hold. That message resonated deeply in my spirit. I knew the situation was beyond my natural ability. I was awestruck that the transplant was a success after all the adversity. How could God know to design the timing of all these connections? He had ordered the universe, and I was set on a journey of purpose and healing. Going in prayer to seek what I could do to help; I received a clear answer in my spirit. Those moments were filled with hope and faith. They were moments of fully trusting God. The chances of us being a transplant match were slim to none, and seeing his health continue to improve was nothing short of miraculous.

These same lessons I brought with me into this next phase of the journey. Even in my grief and loss, I believed I could create some meaning from it. The death of my sister Amber and the heartbreak with my former fiancé were not my end. Amber's pain had been too great for her to bear in her final moments, and she could not see the love within her. I had to reimage a life without her. I grieved the loss of the life and love that I had envisioned with May. May had found love elsewhere and had a child soon after she was married. It was the end of their lives with me, but my life was far from over. I had to love myself enough to move forward. I went to therapy to open my heart to those truths. This was a new page to write upon. It was my "to be continued" in a love note to myself.

I would find purpose in my pain and promise in the process. The uncertainty created space for miracles to happen. Living in the unknown increased the activity of my faith. I had to shake away my fears because they only clouded my hope. In gratitude I could bring forth the sun of miracles and possibilities. Now here I was, living in a new place with an enhanced mission of healing, growth, and discovery. I stood atop a mountain with a symphony below, fireworks lighting up the sky above, feeling a sense of profound peace and purpose. I took that moment to consider it as a celebration of something new. Even though the past still rang in my ears like the boom of exploding lights in the sky, it was far enough behind me that I could create a vision for the future. In fact, the energy of that impact pushed me forward with more urgency. The stage was greater now, and my intention was set on healing for higher purpose.

I ask you now to reflect and write your responses to these questions. This may be particularly difficult. Nonetheless, delve deeply into your personal experiences and insights. Begin to recognize past miracles and foster a more hopeful and proactive outlook for the future.

1. *Think about a time when you experienced or witnessed a miracle in your life. How did it impact you, and what emotions did you feel during that moment?*

2. *Consider a period of uncertainty or difficulty in your life. How did you navigate through it, and what unexpected blessings or positive outcomes emerged from that time?*

3. *Recall a situation where you faced significant grief or loss.*

How were you able to find meaning or purpose from that experience, and how did it shape your perspective on life?

4. *Reflect on a moment when you felt a strong sense of faith or intuition guiding you. What steps did you take to act on that feeling, and what were the results of following your inner guidance?*

5. *In what ways can you cultivate a mindset that expects miracles and possibilities, even during challenging times? How can you actively create space for hope and positive change in your daily life?*

NOTES

New Mission

The next beautiful morning, I prepared for my first day on the new job. It seemed like every day was perfectly sunny in California. Despite spending the last few nights on an air mattress, I was thrilled to settle into my new role. For this corporate-level position, wearing a suit and tie was mandatory. Having served in ministry for years back in Indiana, my wardrobe was well-stocked with suits that had now become my daily uniform. With boundless enthusiasm, I was ready to embark on this new chapter of my leadership journey.

The hospital's CEO had built a solid reputation during his six years in the position. Staff admired and trusted him, and my directive was clear: shadow him and absorb every ounce of his expertise. I attended every meeting, listened in on every call, and delved into state regulations governing hospital operations. These thick binders filled with legalese might have been tedious to study but understanding them was essential. Decisions at this level had far-reaching consequences, and the rules served as both a compass and a safety net, minimizing liabilities and guiding the hospital's mission.

However, this role was far more than deciphering policies. Effective leadership required intentional visibility. An oversized office was not where change happened. Every day, armed with a pen and a small notepad, I toured each unit, greeted staff, and connected with patients. Safety rules permeated every corner, with signs like *Stay with the door* and *Watch the door* posted prominently. Entry required either a key or badge swipe, depending on the section. The hospital's recent expansion added capacity for 50 more patients, starkly contrasting its older facilities.

While I had worked in psychiatric hospitals before, this one was unique. The presence of a full-sized in-ground pool for patients astonished me — a rare oasis of normalcy in an environment defined by strict safety protocols. Patients, dressed in simple shorts and shirts, swam under close supervision. Additionally, a gym with basketball hoops offered another therapeutic outlet, though every feature was scrutinized for safety. Even recreational spaces bore the weight of vigilance.

The daily environment was designed to minimize risks. Showers, toilets, furniture, and even window coverings were thoughtfully constructed to prevent self-harm. Plastic utensils and foam trays replaced metal ones in the cafeteria, while trash cans used paper bags instead of plastic. Patients wore blue paper-like shirts and pants, garments that stripped them of individuality but ensured their safety. Nearly all patients — more than 80% — were admitted involuntarily, navigating the fragile terrain between crisis and care.

In my suit and tie I stood out. Being introduced as "Dr. Rollins" often led to confusion; many patients assumed I was a psychiatrist who could discharge them. Once they discovered I was an administrator, some aired grievances, while others shared personal struggles. I welcomed these interactions: they were an opportunity to listen, to humanize the bureaucratic system, and to ensure their voices didn't go unheard.

Their garments symbolized vulnerability; mine, authority. Yet beneath these uniforms, we shared a common purpose: their recovery. They were fathers, mothers, sons, and daughters, caught in crises, moments of deep emotional pain or enduring chronic illnesses. One patient, a bright-eyed adolescent, had been lost in a system that failed her. Months of bureaucratic indifference eroded her youthful spirit, leaving her stuck in a place that ought to have been her sanctuary. Her story haunted me, a stark reminder of the stakes of leadership in behavioral health.

Staff, while friendly, were vigilant. Technicians patrolled every 15 minutes, clipboards in hand, recording each patient's location and activity with methodical precision. Nurses huddled in small stations; their work consumed by endless documentation in massive binders. Patients noticed. "Why do they spend more time with their papers than with us?" one asked. The question lingered, exposing the tension between administrative demands and the human connection so vital to healing. Compliance required perfection, but at what cost? The binders, filled with colored tabs signaling the next action, seemed to prioritize the process over the people.

I observed group therapy sessions, where patients gathered in hard plastic chairs around plain tables. Some were engaged, while others stared into the distance, lost in their own worlds. One young woman fidgeted with the hem of her shirt, her eyes darting nervously. Later, I learned her story: an involuntary admission after a severe depressive episode. Misdiagnoses and inadequate support had marred her journey through the mental health system. Her experience, like so many others, underscored the profound need for compassionate and competent care.

You have likely heard phrases such as "lead by example" or that "the best leaders are those who know how to follow." The concept of *servant leadership* reinforces this idea, emphasizing that effective leadership is rooted in service to others. Servant leaders build on mutual support and create a shared strength in organizations. They seek to empower others instead of taking power. They stand out in front during adversity to enable their teams to perform through and step back during success to let the light shine on employees that make it possible. This approach helps those in positions of authority engage and inspire people toward a shared mission while fostering trust, collaboration and growth. Are you a servant leader and how do you demonstrate that form of leadership in your daily routine?

This next set of questions is designed for those who hold leadership roles. Leadership is not just about guiding others — it also involves leading and managing your own emotional experiences. Being a courageous decision-maker is essential not only for influencing others but also for navigating the uncertainties of life. True leadership requires both resilience and emotional intelligence, allowing you to transform challenges into opportunities for personal and professional growth.

1. *Think about a time when you were thrust into an unfamiliar role or environment. How did you navigate the challenges, and what helped you endure?*

2. *What tools or strategies do you rely on to maintain resilience during major transitions?*

3. *In your current or past roles, how have you balanced administrative responsibilities with meaningful human connections?*

4. *How do you ensure the people you serve feel seen and valued, even within systems that demand efficiency?*

5. *Consider the symbolism of uniforms in the story — what do*

your garments say about your role and how others perceive you?

6. *How do you use the power you hold, whether in leadership or everyday life, to empower others rather than diminish them?*

7. *Are there aspects of your organization or community that prioritize procedure over people? How might you advocate for change?*

8. *If you've ever felt lost in a system, what did you need most, and how can you offer that to others?*

NOTES

Changing Pace

This was the daily routine. The hospital operated around the clock, a 24-hour haven for those in emotional and psychological pain. Each day, new individuals arrived via ambulance, wheeled in on gurneys, their lives unraveling. Upon arrival, they were checked in with the nursing team, monitored, medicated, and typically discharged within a week. As patients left, their belongings were returned to them in a hospital-issued brown bag.

On the surface, it didn't seem like we were making a profound impact. We caught people at their worst, stabilized their crises and sent them on their way, often uncertain of what lay ahead. Our role in the system was to provide a critical bridge: to help patients regain their footing and connect them with follow-up care. Yet, many left with a fragile grip on stability, walking back into the same storms that had driven them to us.

A common assumption is that psychiatric hospitalization can prevent suicide. The reality is far more complicated. Research shows that the risk of suicide often increases after discharge, especially if follow-up care is delayed (Che, Gwon & Kim, 2023). A delay of more than seven days can exponentially raise the risk of self-harm or worse. And this is precisely where the health-care system often fails.

Who is responsible for bridging this gap? The patient, clutching a brown bag of their belongings, still reeling from the crisis? Their family, grappling with fear and limited resources? The insurance companies, which dictate short stays due to lack of "medical necessity"? The hospital staff, stretched thin yet devoted to patient safety? Or the next provider, overwhelmed with existing clients and weeks-long waiting lists?

The gap between despair and hope is where true challenges lie. Building that stable bridge from the depths of pain to the promise of healing demands more than policies or protocols — it requires heart, resolve and systemic change.

Learning Leadership

Shadowing the hospital CEO became my cornerstone assignment. My first task as COO was to manage leadership meetings. The department heads were a diverse group, each with a distinct style. The nursing director was meticulous and tireless, often stepping in to complete tasks herself. The admissions director guarded her team like a mother hen — fiercely protective and beloved for her empathy. Human Resources followed the rules with a friendly demeanor, while the medical staff was a patchwork of personalities and approaches — some cohesive, others more fractious. It often felt like a family business, complete with its quirks and dysfunctions.

Over a few months, I found my rhythm with the team. I assisted the CEO with special projects aimed at aligning the management departments. I noticed that while department heads had a clear view of their own operations, they often failed to see how the hospital could function more effectively as a whole. When something went wrong, there was a tendency to shift blame onto other departments. Co-workers were friendly, yet an unspoken frustration lingered, subtly impairing collective progress. When tensions rose, staff would retreat into their own lanes, furthering silos instead of bridging them. The CEO frequently acted as a mediator, soothing tempers like a caring parent in the middle of a sibling dispute. He was the stabilizing force for the entire hospital, setting the tone for the organization. No matter the day or hour, he was always on call, ready to handle any crisis. I watched as he navigated the relentless pressures of the corporate entity that dictated his budget and strategic direction.

As the holiday season approached, the hospital prepared for its annual gala: a cherished tradition that even former employees would return to celebrate. But the holidays brought more than just festivities. Near the end of the year, a sentinel event shook the hospital: a young patient died unexpectedly. It was a shock to everyone. She had suffered a medical emergency, and despite all efforts, she did not recover. The exact cause of death was unclear, and an investigation was set to take place. In the immediate aftermath, staff defaulted to finger-pointing, each department scrambling to deflect blame.

Weighed down by the unrelenting pressures of leadership, the CEO reached his breaking point. "I can't do this anymore, Marlon," he confessed, exhaustion etched into his face. He apologized profusely, but his mind was made up — he needed to prioritize his wellbeing and step away before burnout consumed him entirely.

With his departure, I was appointed Interim CEO — a role that carried authority but limited power. The corporate office made it clear: "Just keep everything the same." From their perspective, this hospital was one of the highest revenue-generating locations in the system, and they wanted continuity. But beneath the surface, I could see that the hospital was veering off course, headed straight for trouble.

Crisis Management

One month into my interim role, the California Department of Public Health (CDPH) arrived to investigate the patient death from December. The visit, though expected, felt like a storm breaking over us. Four surveyors entered the hospital with stern expressions, setting up in the conference room like detectives preparing for interrogation. I introduced myself and the Risk and Compliance Director, and together, we braced for what was to come. The team combed through records, policies and conducted interviews with an unwavering focus.

The inquiry exposed the hospital's vulnerabilities with stark clarity. Every layer of our operations — from safety protocols to staff training — was scrutinized. The atmosphere was tense but we knew that transparency was our only option. The surveyors meticulously examined policies, searching for gaps between what was written and what was practiced.

The challenges didn't end there. The following week, The Joint Commission (TJC) arrived for their tri-annual review. Their presence was both a test and an opportunity. I gathered the leadership team to meet the surveyors, striking a balance between formality and an honest acknowledgment of our recent struggles. There was no room for finger-pointing. We had to present a united front and take full accountability.

"We're committed to improvement," I assured them, presenting evidence of our efforts to address deficiencies. The surveyors appreciated our honesty and our willingness to learn from adversity. Their guidance became a beacon, reinforcing our resolve to rebuild trust and demonstrate the integrity of our care.

We were reassured by their approach, yet we knew we couldn't let our guard down. Protecting the hospital's credibility required full ownership of any problems. The TJC surveyors methodically reviewed our policies and procedures, evaluating how they aligned with actual practice. Despite our imperfections, we ensured that every document was thoroughly vetted before handing it over, hoping our commitment to progress would be evident.

By the second day, the survey had yielded few surprises. But on the third day, the situation escalated dramatically. CDPH officials returned — this time under the authority of the Centers for Medicare & Medicaid Services (CMS). Without hesitation, CMS representatives confronted the TJC surveyors, demanding that the accreditation review be halted. Because our hospital's state license was under scrutiny, CMS asserted that licensing took precedence over accreditation. The tension was palpable. The TJC team was stunned when they were asked to leave the building.

With CMS now leading the investigation, the stakes were far higher. They aggressively probed every aspect of the hospital's operations, conducting in-depth patient interviews and scouring additional records, determined to uncover any deficiencies.

Then, in the midst of it all, a crisis unfolded: a patient attempted suicide in the restroom. The individual, frantic to avoid discharge, had made a desperate choice. It was a catastrophic moment, reinforcing the urgency of our situation. I felt like a captain trying to stabilize a ship that kept crashing into rocks.

At the conclusion of their investigation, CMS issued over 140 citations and placed the hospital on immediate jeopardy status: a federal designation signaling that patient safety was at severe risk. If we didn't correct the deficiencies within 20 days, the hospital could be forced to close. The impact was swift and far-reaching. TJC placed us on preliminary denial of accreditation, meaning our accreditation would be permanently revoked if the license was lost. The hospital's future, along with hundreds of jobs, hung in the balance.

Word spread quickly among local partners and insurance providers, further compounding the crisis. The hospital, one of the Bay Area's largest mental health facilities, served more than 120 adults and adolescents at any given time. CMS mandated an immediate halt to new admissions and required all staff to undergo emergency response retraining. The ripple effects were devastating — not just for our hospital but for the entire mental health system in the region. Emergency departments that relied on us had nowhere to send psychiatric patients. The disruption threatened to destabilize the entire network of care.

This was the reality of leadership in crisis: navigating a regulatory minefield while holding a health-care team together. The corporate office dispatched senior leaders to assist, which I appreciated, but their presence only heightened staff anxiety. To many, they felt like yet another layer of scrutiny. Meanwhile, I worked closely with our team of fifteen psychiatrists and physicians, many of whom had been practicing for decades. They were deeply concerned about the impact on their careers and reputations.

During this period, I had to summon every ounce of strength I had. The demands were relentless: 10-hour days on-site, followed by on-call responsibilities around the clock. There was no room for error. If another incident occurred, the consequences would be dire. Every process needed to be expedited, every policy scrutinized. Patient documentation, which was still entirely paper-based, had to be meticulously reviewed and updated. Staff had to learn new forms and protocols overnight.

One moment in particular stayed with me. The head of the CMS team pulled me aside after identifying even more problems. I felt a wave of embarrassment as she spoke.

"The nursing staff is not empowered," she told me bluntly. As a regulatory nurse, she saw the issue as deeper than paperwork or policy — it was about culture. "They need to be able to make decisions with confidence. They have to know they're supported when they act in the best interest of patients."

Her words resonated. I had already heard patient complaints that nurses seemed more focused on documentation than actual care. When patients felt unheard or ignored, the system was failing them.

I refocused my efforts on empowering the nursing staff, fostering a culture where they could make informed decisions without fear. True change, I realized, had to start with leadership. We needed to restore clarity and confidence in the hospital—despite the chaos. The actions you take as a servant leader set the tone and allow others to show up in their strength and creativity. To try to do it all or run the show makes the transformation temporary because it is limited only to you. A growing successful organization is made of growing courageous people.

In those moments, I learned that leadership wasn't just about policies and procedures. It was about presence. As I walked the hospital's halls, I became acutely aware that my demeanor set the tone. People watched my face for reassurance, searching for signs that things would be okay. The truth was, I didn't know if they would be. But every day, I carried the weight of ensuring that my team felt supported, that patients felt safe, and that the hospital could withstand the storm.

For the nursing staff, this was more than just a job — it was their livelihood, their identity. Many feared that their association with the hospital might jeopardize their licenses. They needed reassurance, a sense of stability in the chaos. I knew that if fear ruled the workplace, healing would be impossible.

This was the test of leadership and transformation: holding a team together under immense pressure, guiding them through uncertainty, and making decisions that would determine the future of the hospital, its staff, and the patients who depended on us. If you are in a leadership role or are an aspiring leader, take a moment to answer these questions. We can only take others as far as we are willing to go ourselves in good will.

1. *In times of crisis, what strategies do you use to regain stability and maintain focus? Can you identify the "bridges" in your life that help you transition from pain to purpose?*

2. *How do you navigate moments when your authority feels limited, yet the stakes are high? What role does transparency play in your decision-making?*

3. *Have you experienced a situation where a system or process failed to meet your needs? What steps could you take—or have taken—to address those gaps?*

4. *How do you measure the impact of your efforts, even when results seem fleeting or intangible?*

5. *Think of a time when you were thrown into a challenging role with little preparation. How did you rise to meet the demands, and what did you learn about your capacity for growth?*

NOTES

Transforming Fear into Action

At the outset, fear was our primary motivator. The looming consequences of inaction kept us on edge. But fear alone couldn't sustain a health-care team—it would inevitably lead to burnout. The pressure weighed on every member of the executive team. We didn't have the luxury of blaming each other or individual departments for mistakes. Instead, we had to find solutions.

To fill gaps in our knowledge, I reached out to professionals at sister hospitals, learning about best practices and how to incorporate them into our own operations. I won't deny that a part of me wanted to prove I could be just as effective as the CEO. But I wasn't arrogant enough to think I had all the answers. I certainly didn't. Pretending otherwise would have been disingenuous. Instead, I leaned into communication, increasing my presence and engagement with the team.

I met with staff individually when they needed extra support, conducted unit rounds, and held town hall meetings. Turning things around required an all-hands-on-deck approach, and my role as the newly-appointed leader was to ensure everyone was on board with the changes. Transparency and accountability were non-negotiable.

Finger-pointing was a significant barrier to progress. Staff members deflected criticism onto other departments — physicians blamed nurses, nurses blamed doctors, and the admissions office was accused of bringing in the wrong patients. This cycle of blame prevented improvement and put everyone's jobs at risk. Our rallying cry became one of unity: we had to build each other up, not tear each other down.

For real change to happen, doctors had to actively participate in and financially support nurse education programs. Communication had to evolve beyond simply speaking—we had to listen to one another. The way directives were issued also had to shift. Nurses were empowered to act in the best interest of patients first and inform doctors afterward, minimizing unnecessary delays. Taking responsibility for our actions toward one another became a guiding principle.

We focused on transforming frustration and fear into actionable steps for improvement. Collaboration was no longer optional — it was essential. Our goal was to turn setbacks into opportunities for growth. This meant revising paperwork and records to reflect improved procedures, but more importantly, it required tangible, daily teamwork. Change couldn't just exist in policies and documentation; it had to be felt in every patient interaction.

Patient safety became a shared responsibility. But for staff to keep patients safe, they first needed to feel secure in their roles and equipped to handle crises. Mistakes were inevitable, but they had to be learning experiences rather than hidden failures. Fear of repercussions only led to bigger disasters.

One critical change involved our emergency response procedures. Previously, in a unit emergency, designated staff from various levels of the hospital were supposed to arrive at the scene with specific emergency equipment. However, if someone was busy with a patient or didn't notice the alert, vital equipment could be forgotten. Transporting supplies through key-restricted elevators and long hallways was inefficient and prone to errors.

We replaced this system with fully-stocked emergency carts on every unit, eliminating the need for last-minute equipment retrieval. A specialized emergency response team was deployed daily, and all employees were trained in effective crisis communication and task delegation. To reinforce these protocols, we ran frequent drills, tracking response times and testing staff on how to handle specific medical scenarios. The nursing director conducted in-person training sessions, ensuring staff knew exactly what to do in an emergency. Every step related to patient safety was analyzed, refined, and reinforced through hands-on practice.

Change wasn't easy, but it was necessary. The mindset of "this is how we've always done it" was no longer acceptable. Resistance to change was a fundamental issue — we couldn't grow without evolving. Progress required adaptation, and adaptation required learning.

Most importantly, we had to learn from one another.

A Test of Resilience and Leadership

After five months of relentless effort our team began making meaningful progress, steadily reporting improvements to public health authorities. Then, in late May, my boss informed me that the company planned to hire a more experienced CEO to replace me. I was disheartened. I had worked tirelessly alongside my team to navigate a regulatory nightmare, only to be told that a seasoned executive would be more appealing to the licensing authorities. Despite my objections, I had no choice but to comply. Senior leadership warned me that if things deteriorated further, they didn't want me in the line of fire due to the high stakes involved.

The newly appointed CEO was intelligent and professional, yet he struggled to earn the trust of the team. Unlike me, he hadn't endured the challenges we faced or been in the trenches pushing for change. Many of my colleagues viewed his appointment as a betrayal; an injustice given my dedication and perseverance. I won't deny it — my initial reaction was frustration. Working seven days a week, only to have the mantle passed to someone else, felt like an insult. I wrestled with self-reflection, grappling with the reality that, in the eyes of upper management, I still had to prove my worth.

By July, I realized that I had gone an entire year without a single day off. The chaos had consumed me. It was time to step back. With a new CEO in place, I finally allowed myself to take a vacation; both to recharge and to give him the space to lead without my presence overshadowing his authority. I needed to ensure the leadership transition was stable.

To mark the four-year anniversary of donating a kidney to my father, I took him on our first-ever trip to Hawaii. I had envisioned it as a paradise, but it became something more — an essential moment of clarity. Over the past several months, I had allowed myself to be consumed by the need to prove myself. I had sacrificed my well-being, convinced that my worth was tied to a title. But in Hawaii, I accepted that I was not the CEO. If the role was meant for me, my time would come. What mattered most was the impact I had made and the lives I had helped improve.

Four days into my vacation, I received a call from the regional supervisor. The state licensing team had returned to the hospital for another evaluation. My first instinct was to find a way back to help. Had I been anywhere else, I might have cut my trip short. But being on an island created a physical barrier that forced me to stay put. I had to trust the leadership in place to handle the situation. At that moment, I knew I needed to release myself from the weight of responsibility.

However, when I returned, I learned that things had not gone as planned. The inspectors were dissatisfied with the progress, and new conflicts had emerged over licensing. This time, they scrutinized dietary services and patient nutrition. Our Medicare eligibility was now at risk. If Medicare funding was cut, every other insurance provider would follow, leading to financial collapse. We would no longer be able to accept insured patients — a terrifying thought. Despite the hospital's recent financial success, none of it mattered if we couldn't maintain quality care.

It was clear that if we were going to overcome this final hurdle, our teamwork needed to improve. My new objective as COO was to provide stronger support to the CEO. I recommitted myself to the team, working alongside leadership to secure the necessary resources. Over time, the CEO and I built a mutual respect: he came to rely on me for operational improvements. Together, we addressed the additional concerns raised by regulators, modifying policies, updating procedures, and reinforcing training programs. Directors provided real-time training, and I continued holding town halls to instill hope and maintain morale.

This was our last stand. We worked tirelessly to ensure the hospital was running smoothly. When the final review day arrived, we passed. By the end of the year, we had made significant improvements, lifting a tremendous weight off our shoulders. The division president personally visited me to express gratitude for my endurance. We celebrated as a team, and for the first time in a long while, I felt validated.

But leadership in health-care is unpredictable. A few weeks later, the CEO returned from a budget meeting with new goals for the coming year. Then, without warning, he was fired. One morning, as I pulled into the hospital parking lot, I saw him leaving with a small box of his belongings, his head hanging low. The following week, the CFO was also dismissed.

Once again, I was named interim CEO. But this time, the promotion felt different. Instead of excitement, I felt doubt. Was this even the position I wanted?

I began to sense the unsettling reality of leadership in a high-stakes environment. It was not just lonely; it was unstable. One misstep, and you could be replaced without warning. The phrase I heard so often rang in my ears: "*Execute or be executed.*" In the corporate world of health-care, if something went wrong, someone had to take the fall.

I had fought to prove my worth. But now, I had to ask myself: was this the kind of leadership I wanted to pursue?

A New Chapter in Leadership

Despite the ongoing challenges, the staff remained supportive, and I deeply appreciated their resilience and teamwork. Efforts to reorganize the hospital's financial performance continued, and an interim CFO was appointed. Although time had passed since our initial denial, we were still awaiting a visit from the Joint Commission. Meanwhile, we successfully cleared CMS, yet it felt as if corporate leadership had launched an all-out offensive following the sudden resignations of the CEO and CFO.

The focus remained firmly on financial recovery. While we were treating and admitting patients, rebuilding trust with the community and referring partners became essential. Competition in the area was intensifying as similar hospitals emerged. Public perception and market positioning had become the new challenges.

After nearly two years with the organization and still being passed over for a permanent leadership role, I began questioning my future there. Corporate leadership assured me that, once I completed my training as COO, they would place me in charge of a smaller hospital. The offer felt patronizing. Still, I understood they relied on me to provide stability amid the turmoil. However, I knew I needed to explore other opportunities.

Once I made my job search public, a recruiter contacted me about a COO position at a leading addiction treatment center in Southern California. In just three years, the facility had built a national reputation for excellence, backed by clinical research and a published white paper on treatment outcomes. The opportunity to work with a specialized, competitive program excited me. At my current hospital, addiction was not a primary focus, even though many patients suffering from substance abuse required mental health intervention. While we could stabilize them through detox, we lacked the resources to address the root causes of their addiction. It was an element that reminded me of my sister's treatment that had fallen short.

Eager to explore this new role, I took a long weekend off for the interview. The CEO personally arranged my travel, covering my airfare and lodging. He even extended his generosity to my father, inviting him along for the trip. He encouraged me to spend the weekend exploring the area, familiarizing myself with the community and its housing options. It was a thoughtful introduction to what could be a meaningful collaboration.

The interview process was thorough, as expected for an executive position. The leadership team asked in-depth questions about my experience and motivations. I shared my journey, my passion for transformative leadership, and my desire to create lasting change in behavioral health-care. The CEO, in turn, shared his vision for the hospital and his need for a strategic partner to help drive growth. The possibility of contributing to something innovative and patient-centered was invigorating.

While I awaited their decision, I returned to my role as interim CEO. After a turbulent year, the path forward at my current job remained unclear, reinforcing my need for a backup plan. I had always envisioned staying in California, yet no viable opportunities were emerging. Senior executives rarely disclosed their retirement plans, leaving me in professional limbo. Planning for the future became increasingly difficult.

I remained committed to making a meaningful impact, but I couldn't shake the feeling that the company was positioning itself to replace me with a more seasoned CEO. My instincts proved correct. A senior executive's trusted colleague introduced me — outside of work — to the company's new CEO. When asked to assist with onboarding, I agreed. However, when word spread that I was being temporarily removed from my role, the response was overwhelming.

Employees were outraged. Doctors rallied to my defense. Many of them had supported me in rebuilding the hospital, and their loyalty was deeply moving. Community liaisons also expressed their gratitude, reinforcing that my leadership had made a tangible difference. Through internal surveys, I confirmed what I already knew: as CEO, I was accountable not just to corporate leadership but to the people who relied on me every day.

In reality, I had never been meant to serve as the permanent CEO. I was a stabilizer, a trainer. The challenges I had faced had prepared me for adversity and uncertainty. But I also learned that leadership isn't just about guiding others — it's about managing your own identity. Executive roles come with an emotional toll, and I became acutely aware of the risks of compassion fatigue.

One of the most valuable lessons I took away was the necessity of self-care in fostering courageous leadership. Leadership demands decisiveness. In moments of crisis, it's better to make an informed decision than to do nothing. It's unwise to bear the burden alone — seeking counsel in difficult times is essential. And above all, I realized that people crave connection. No matter the outcome, employees want to feel valued, heard and included.

As a servant leader, I took my responsibility seriously. I ensured the incoming CEO had all the information needed to succeed. I briefed her on the hospital's history, the management team's initiatives, and the strengths and opportunities ahead. It felt like the peaceful transition of power in a presidential inauguration. Though I had poured my heart into leading the hospital, I knew that the future direction was now in her hands.

Letting go was difficult. But my journey was not over. I was soon reassigned to work under a seasoned CEO in Sacramento; a leader I greatly respected. He had guided his hospital through its darkest times and expanded it into one of California's largest health-care facilities. I looked forward to learning from his steady leadership.

Just a week into my new position, I received a call from my former hospital. The Joint Commission had returned to resurvey the facility to overturn the preliminary denial. This was the final hurdle. Understanding the stakes, I immediately informed my new CEO and made the two-hour drive back to assist my former team.

The accreditation process was a critical validation of the hospital's commitment to patient safety and quality care. As I arrived, the survey was just beginning. I provided the new CEO with a comprehensive briefing, ensuring she could effectively advocate for the hospital's progress over the past year.

This moment belonged to the leadership team. They had

worked tirelessly, and now they had the opportunity to showcase their growth. I shifted into a supportive role, offering encouragement rather than direct leadership. Watching them rise to the challenge filled me with pride. By the second day of the survey, it was clear they were well-prepared to succeed.

Then, the final confirmation arrived. The head nurse called to deliver the news: after reviewing past deficiencies against present improvements, the surveyors declared a complete turnaround.

They had done it. The hospital had passed its accreditation review. The long, hard battle was over.

Embracing Change and New Opportunities

Being part of such a monumental achievement brought immense satisfaction. As a leader, I had learned the importance of allowing my team to take credit for their successes while shielding them from the full brunt of setbacks, giving them space to grow. With this accreditation secured, the hospital was in a much stronger position, better equipped to face future challenges. The experience had been fulfilling and transformative, but uncertainty still lingered over my career.

The Southern California hospital had yet to follow up, and as summer drew to a close, I turned my focus to supporting the CEO of my newly-assigned hospital. My role involved strengthening the expanding outpatient programs while observing a seasoned executive in action. The inpatient team was solid: while challenges existed, every staff member understood their role and contributed effectively. The hospital treated more than 150 patients daily, with approximately 25 new admissions each day. Drawing from my past leadership experiences, I dedicated my efforts to enhancing the outpatient network and preparing for the upcoming Joint

Commission survey.

Meanwhile, I waited to hear about a nearby hospital searching for a CEO. The uncertainty made it difficult to make personal plans; I feared being uprooted and forced to start over elsewhere. The CEO I was working under remained active at the regional level, frequently visiting different sites. His mentorship was one of the main reasons I had joined the company; his insights into business operations and strategic management had been invaluable. However, a clear pathway for my advancement within the organization remained elusive.

Then, three months into my new role, I finally heard back from the Southern California addiction treatment center. The recruiter asked if I was still interested in the COO position. Why not? In many ways, I had already been performing the responsibilities of a COO. By this point, I had shed any attachment to titles — what mattered most was making a meaningful impact. I told her I'd like to be considered if the position became available.

That's when she dropped an unexpected update: the CEO I had previously interviewed with had been fired. They now wanted me to meet with the newly appointed CEO. The news took me by surprise, but I understood the necessity. I agreed and scheduled a call.

During our conversation, the new CEO — despite his extensive health-care background — expressed his excitement about having a strong and reliable COO to support him in his new role. His enthusiasm reassured me, and the leadership transition gave me hope that the organization was stabilizing. The program was expanding, serving both Orange County and San Diego. My role would involve strengthening operations, resolving regulatory challenges that had persisted since the hospital's inception, and aligning the treatment continuum between the two locations.

Something about this opportunity felt right. I had the impression that they valued my expertise and were prepared to offer a significantly higher salary. The scope of work aligned perfectly with my skills and aspirations.

When I informed my current CEO of my decision, he was disappointed but not surprised, given everything I had endured at my previous hospital. He acknowledged that the salary increase was substantial and supported my move. His encouragement meant a great deal to me.

I provided a month's notice to ensure a smooth transition, passing along pending projects to the appropriate team members. Colleagues were understanding and appreciative of the time we had spent working together. The decision felt right, and I looked forward to the next chapter.

A Journey Through Change and Leadership

With excitement and anticipation, I packed my belongings and set out on the long journey from Sacramento to Orange County, ready to embrace new challenges and opportunities. Moving southward from Northern California's pine forests to Southern California's palm-lined coastlines brought a dramatic shift in climate and scenery. I felt a deeper connection to the ocean, captivated by its hypnotic sunsets. Joining a thriving business in such a picturesque location felt like an exciting new chapter.

Understanding my role within the organization, I made it a point to invest in the publicly traded company. The CEO frequently visited each site via private jet, demonstrating a deep interest in both treatment quality and operational performance. His level of involvement and the company's success were inspiring, fueling my motivation to contribute to its expansion. However, I couldn't ignore the unsettling reality that the first CEO I had met had been fired. Still, I resolved to focus on the opportunity before me, dedicating myself to strengthening operations and supporting the new CEO's strategic vision.

That optimism was soon tested. About one month after onboarding, we were informed by the President and COO of upcoming strategic budget cuts aimed at reducing overhead expenses. One of the most difficult decisions was the closure of the San Diego program. While I was disappointed, my feelings paled in comparison to the distress of the affected employees. Contrary to my expectations, I spent the next 30 days dismantling operations, standing alongside the CEO as we delivered the news. As a shareholder, I also witnessed a decline in my personal investment in the company. Restoring financial stability while maintaining quality care became the pressing concern.

A regulatory monitor had been overseeing the treatment center since its inception, yet the facility had not been cleared. As COO, I focused on bringing the necessary expertise to resolve this issue while also implementing cost-saving measures that wouldn't compromise service quality. One glaring inefficiency stood out: laundry services. The hospital, which accommodated up to 90 patients at a time, spent more than $20,000 monthly on outsourcing linens and personal clothing. The process was cumbersome: patients often discharged before receiving their laundry, leading to complaints and logistical challenges. My solution was to install commercial-grade laundry equipment on every floor, reducing costs to just $500 per month by leasing equipment and outsourcing maintenance. This streamlined process ensured that patients' belongings remained within the facility until their discharge.

Over the next year, I worked with the team to refine operations. We successfully cleared the regulatory monitor and assembled a strong clinical and compliance team. However, the company continued to cut staff in an effort to save costs. The CEO, committed to retaining jobs, took a bottom-up approach to expense reduction. Even the private jet flights came to an end. By late 2019, I witnessed yet another leadership transition as the CEO was dismissed. Then, in early 2020, I was appointed CEO.

The promotion was an honor, but it came with apprehension. The revolving door of leadership had shown me the precarious nature of the role — CEOs were the first to go when things went wrong. Behavioral health and addiction treatment were ever-evolving fields, and the weight of responsibility was immense. I entered the new year with cautious optimism, but as the world would soon learn, 2020 had unprecedented challenges in store.

The COVID-19 pandemic hit swiftly, altering the landscape of health-care. Travel restrictions disrupted patient admissions, further straining the company's financial stability. Our task force mobilized to develop isolation and quarantine protocols. As PPE shortages gripped the nation, we sourced handmade masks and bulk-ordered hand sanitizer. The hospital, with its shared cafeteria, pool, and group therapy sessions, required significant restructuring to ensure safety while maintaining therapeutic integrity.

In the midst of our pandemic response, the company filed for Chapter 11 bankruptcy. Uncertainty loomed over employees who feared for their jobs. I held daily virtual town halls, aiming to provide transparency and reassurance despite the lack of concrete answers. These meetings became a support system, fostering collective problem-solving and solidarity. Staff showed remarkable resilience, continuing to provide critical care despite their own fears.

Then, our worst fear materialized: a patient tested positive for COVID-19. As the CEO, I made the decision to personally escort them to an isolation facility, ensuring a safe and controlled transfer. Soon, the virus spread among staff and patients, infecting nearly 30 individuals. A beloved team member, exhausted from battling the outbreak, fell ill and had to be hospitalized. The situation escalated as holiday travel increased infections, and some patients, driven by fear, even threatened legal action.

Leading through both a pandemic and a corporate bankruptcy was a test of endurance. Just as we began to see the light at the end of the tunnel, I received a call from corporate HR. The newly appointed CEO of the parent company informed me, "Thank you for your work during COVID-19, but we are going in another direction." Stunned, I felt myself shrink in the room. I asked them to repeat what he just said. In that moment, I understood I was being let go. The very fate I had sought to avoid had found me. I was given a separation package, but the reality was clear: my tenure had come to an end. My heart sank in my chest, grasping for a rebuttal. It was like being pushed off a cliff after making it to the top of the mountain only to catch a glimpse of the view. My words of plea were as though I was grabbing falling rocks to save myself from the fall. With no further regard, my job was done there.

Shortly after my departure, tragedy struck — our employee who had fallen ill passed away. The weight of loss was profound. He lost his life, while I had merely lost my job. The emotions were overwhelming. 2020 had been defined by crisis — global upheaval, social unrest, financial collapse, and health-care disruptions. And now, I faced my own uncertainty. For the first time in years, I found myself without a defined role or direction.

In moments of loss, I turned to faith. The ocean became my sanctuary — the rhythmic waves calming my restless thoughts. One December morning, as the sun broke through the clouds, I prayed. I laid out my fears and frustrations before God. And in that moment of stillness, clarity emerged: I had time to write.

For the first time in what felt like an eternity, I had no immediate obligations. I channeled my energy into a long-held aspiration: writing my first book. *Healing the Impoverished Mind: Building Resilience Through Adversity* was born. The process of writing helped me to find meaning in my journey. By reflecting on my experiences, I uncovered a deeper purpose. My book became a memoir of resilience, a testimony to overcoming hardship, and a beacon of hope for others navigating adversity.

What had initially felt like an end was, in truth, a new beginning — a new chapter.

Navigating Leadership Transitions

Before my first book was released in 2021, I landed a new position as the Chief Executive Officer of a drug and alcohol treatment center with locations in Newport Beach and Riverside. This center had been in operation for several decades but had recently been acquired by a larger organization. From the outset, I had concerns about its infrastructure — astonishingly, in 2021, all patient records were still kept on paper. Managing multiple treatment sites without a modernized system created significant operational inefficiencies. Still, this was my new challenge.

Early conversations with staff revealed a troubling pattern: previous CEOs were largely absent, either physically or in leadership presence. Some rarely showed up at all. I was stunned that a health-care facility could function with such a detached approach, and I made it clear that I would operate differently.

As I evaluated the programs, it became apparent that leadership confidence was lacking. Despite their dedication, the managers had little strategic direction or managerial expertise. Clinical services were inconsistent, and some facilities showed signs of failing. The organization barely passed its CARF (Commission on Accreditation of Rehabilitation Facilities) survey, relying on hastily compiled documentation from the previous three years. At the time of the evaluation, I had only been in my role for two months. While we met the minimum standards for accreditation, it was clear that the program was being held together with duct tape.

Determined to create lasting change, I worked closely with the directors and leveraged my experience with regulatory bodies like the Joint Commission. We transitioned from paper records to an electronic health record system and spent the following year refining and elevating the program to meet the highest industry standards. However, significant changes in corporate leadership soon created instability.

The CEO of the parent company — a leader with decades of experience — announced her retirement, setting off a domino effect of turnover. Within a year, three different supervisors in my reporting chain either resigned or were replaced. As the turbulence escalated, I made a conscious decision to prioritize environments that offered stability and a clear path forward. When the right opportunity presented itself, I resigned voluntarily. For the first time in a long while, I felt I was making a choice that aligned with both my professional values and personal well-being. I had enough experience at this to determine what was required and what is in my desire to build. I had to wrestle with my ego wanting to fix everything and sacrificing myself in the process.

A year later, the corporation never appointed a permanent CEO. One by one, its operations unraveled — first in Riverside, then in Newport Beach. Though I had long since moved on, it was hard to learn the corporation shut it all down. Nevertheless, I was grateful for the relationships I had built during my tenure, and some have remained good friends.

Stepping into Transformational Leadership

After leaving that role, another opportunity emerged — this time with a privately owned organization. Unlike the corporate structure I had just left, this company had been founded and run by a tight-knit group of entrepreneurs. They were looking for a transformational leader to take charge of their newly-formed alcohol and drug treatment division. Over the previous five years, they had grown substantially, but they lacked the structure needed to sustain their expansion.

Over the course of six months, I implemented a strategic framework that aligned the division with the organization's broader mission. The results were so impactful that leadership reconsidered their initial plan to sell off parts of the company. Instead, they asked me to stay on as President and Chief Operating Officer to replicate this success across their mental health service lines.

Coaching the leadership team and helping them build capacity was incredibly rewarding. However, as operations stabilized, my role became less critical. As a high-level executive, my continued presence became an unnecessary expense. Recognizing this, I had open and candid discussions with the founders, helping them craft strategic plans to further strengthen the company's future. My work there was complete, and I began searching for my next opportunity to make a difference.

A Hard Lesson in Due Diligence

Two and a half years into that job, I was approached by another company with a promising opportunity. This time, the focus was on mental health services in Orange County—a market I knew well from a prior company that closed. From the start, I was clear with the CEO and co-founders about my expectations: I wanted to build a program with sustainable, long-term growth.

I did my research before joining, but in hindsight, I ought to have dug deeper. About six weeks into my onboarding, I received an early-morning call from the primary investor. His voice was heavy with regret as he explained that the program was in deeper financial distress than initially disclosed. He could no longer justify continued funding. Effective immediately, he was requesting a staff furlough and a suspension of operations.

I was stunned. This went against everything we had discussed during my hiring process. He apologized sincerely, acknowledging that this was not the outcome any of us had wanted. Despite my deep disappointment, I agreed to organize a small core group in navigating the fallout.

No one was spared — not even the CEO. Having once been in his position, I understood the weight of what he was facing. As the remaining team members looked to me for guidance, I once again found myself leading through crisis. Transparency was my priority. I spoke openly with employees and clients, even as it sparked frustration and anger. My immediate focus became ensuring a smooth transition: transferring patients to a trusted facility and helping staff find new employment. Grateful for a professional network and trusted colleagues in the area, we were able to place many employees in new roles. It was the opposite of what I had envisioned what I would be there to do but it was the assignment handed to me.

By the end of 2024, all operations had ceased. And just like that, I found myself back in what I called the "employment valley."

A Vision of My Own

Sitting by the ocean, reflecting on the past years, I recognized a pattern. I had gained invaluable experience — navigating corporate instability, restructuring organizations, and leading teams through uncertainty. But beyond those challenges, I saw the deeper issue: the mental health-care system itself was fragmented, inconsistent, and often failing the very people it was meant to serve.

At every institution I stepped into, I found myself fixing, stabilizing, and filling the gaps. But I kept asking: was I moving toward something, or running away from something? Since arriving in California, had I been chasing purpose, or was I trying to escape pain?

In many ways, I had spent my career trying to redeem what was lost with my sister. The failures of a system that allows people with mental health struggles and addictions to slip through the cracks haunted me. And so, at each organization, I asked the same questions:

- *Did we do the best we could?*
- *Did we learn from our mistakes?*
- *Did we serve people with integrity?*
- *Did we empathize with their pain, or did we judge them?*
- *Did we communicate with their loved ones with kindness, or did we ignore and dismiss them?*

I wanted to be on the right side of these questions. Not just for the patients and clients, but for the employees — the ones who gave their time, energy and hearts in service to these organizations and companies. Purpose wasn't just in the mission statement; it lived in the daily mindset and behaviors of those who carried the mission forward. Where there was division, there was risk. Where there was unity, there was strength.

For a moment, I questioned myself: *Was I broken? Was all of this just an attempt to fix myself?* But then, clarity struck.

I didn't need to fix someone else's system. And I wasn't broken. I was surviving. I was resilient. Every challenge, every setback, every painful lesson had forged me into someone stronger. Each adversity wasn't a weight dragging me down: it was momentum pushing me toward a higher potential.

I wasn't meant to patch up flawed institutions. I was meant to build something of my own.

For the first time, I saw a future that wasn't dictated by corporate shakeups, investor priorities, or reactive decision-making. I had the knowledge, the experience, and — most importantly — the vision to create something meaningful. Something resilient and to inspire others.

It was no longer about whether I held the title of CEO or not. My purpose wasn't confined to a position. To lead was to live with intention. *To be fully present, to embrace the journey, to appreciate everything that had brought me to this moment.* No longer seeking validation, approval, or status — only alignment with the deeper mission that had been guiding me all along.

Resilience isn't just about overcoming obstacles — it's about discovering a greater meaning within yourself. It's about understanding what it takes to sustain your highest potential and creating something that truly lasts.

As we stand on the threshold of pain and uncertainty, we often question whether we possess the capacity to endure and emerge stronger. This journey is not solely about grit or sheer willpower; it is fundamentally about transformation.

Various measures of resilience have been developed to quantify this capacity. Tools like the Brief Resilient Coping Scale (BRCS), the Connor-Davidson Resilience Scale (CD-RISC), and the State-Trait Assessment of Resilience (STARS) aim to assess an individual's ability to bounce back from adversity. These instruments often rely on self-reported data, providing insights into specific traits associated with resilience. However, self-report measures can sometimes lack depth, offering only a surface-level understanding of a person's resilience.

Beyond personal assessments, resilience is also evaluated on a broader, systemic level. The Resilience Index Measurement and Analysis (RIMA), used by food and agriculture organizations, assesses food insecurity and the capacity of communities or households to recover from natural disasters. This index examines critical systems—such as access to power, water, transportation, and income generation—to determine how well a community can restore its functionality after a crisis.

Similarly, our personal resilience is multifaceted. It encompasses not just our internal attributes but also the external systems that support us. While we are inherently designed for survival, the very mechanisms that protect us during adversity can sometimes hinder our ability to rebound and thrive. Compounding adversity, if not transformed through intentional growth, can break our spirit and confine us to a state of minimal potential.

This is where the concept of Growth Codes comes into play. The Growth Codes are designed to illuminate the internal attributes that influence our resilience. Their objective is to raise awareness and guide us in shifting from a survival mindset to one of thriving. By unlocking these codes, we can begin to transcend our limitations and move toward our maximum potential; transforming adversity into a catalyst for growth and empowerment.

NOTES

Chapter 4

The Codes for Growth

TO ASSIST YOU IN ANSWERING THE QUESTION "ARE YOU prepared for adversity?" this book introduces the Growth Codes. Problems arise in life no matter how hard we try to escape them. People often tell us to "Stay ready!" Suggesting that we ought to always be vigilant and ready for any difficulty. To be properly prepared, though, what does this entail? What does it mean to "get" ready when you don't feel prepared?

This popular proverb frequently suggests a state of perpetual alertness, a state of preparedness that arises from expecting difficulties. However, it might be draining to remain on high alert forever. The Growth Codes do not aim to have its adherents constantly on high alert. Instead, you may use these codes to cultivate a grounded and resilient readiness that will allow you to reach your full potential without sacrificing your health. The goal is to strengthen your resilience so that you can overcome challenges and emerge stronger than before.

Think of a rubber band. Tension is produced when you stretch it. This stress is a kind of potential energy that can be released in response to force or motion. Bands that are either too brittle or too stiff won't be able to extend very far before snapping. However, tremendous latent energy can be stored in the band if its strength and flexibility are optimally balanced. How well a rubber band can stretch and hold depends on its composition and state.

Our ability to adapt and grow follows the same logic. Rather than focusing on being ready for a specific event, the Growth Codes encourage you to tap into your boundless energy and potential so that you can respond with impact in any given situation. Never forget that energy has no limit. The principle of conservation of energy states that energy can only be converted and not created or destroyed. This means that there is an endless potential for the transformation of the energy within us. Take into consideration that your thoughts are energy in and of themselves. Feeling physically exhausted even when you're not moving about is a common symptom of overthinking and worrying.

Efficiency is a crucial component of resilience. Everything is done with a purpose, and every resource is used to its full potential, resulting in maximum efficiency. In this view, resilience is about more than simply getting back up; it's also about getting back up with less effort and more impact. Efficiently recovering from setbacks is resilience. Higher resilience is the ability to swiftly recover from disturbances and resume optimal behavior.

Though fictitious, consider the Vibranium suit worn by the superhero Black Panther. In the film, Black Panther can unleash his superhuman strength by storing the energy from every attack that the suit absorbs. This process exemplifies resilience by converting energy — even energy that could be harmful — into something beneficial.

In most cases, testing is the only way to determine an object's resilience. We tend to wait until something, or someone, has actually gone through adversity before we call them resilient. True resilience, however, can and ought to be developed in advance.

The Growth Codes advise laying the groundwork for resilience, which will serve you well through tough times and allow you to come out stronger than before.

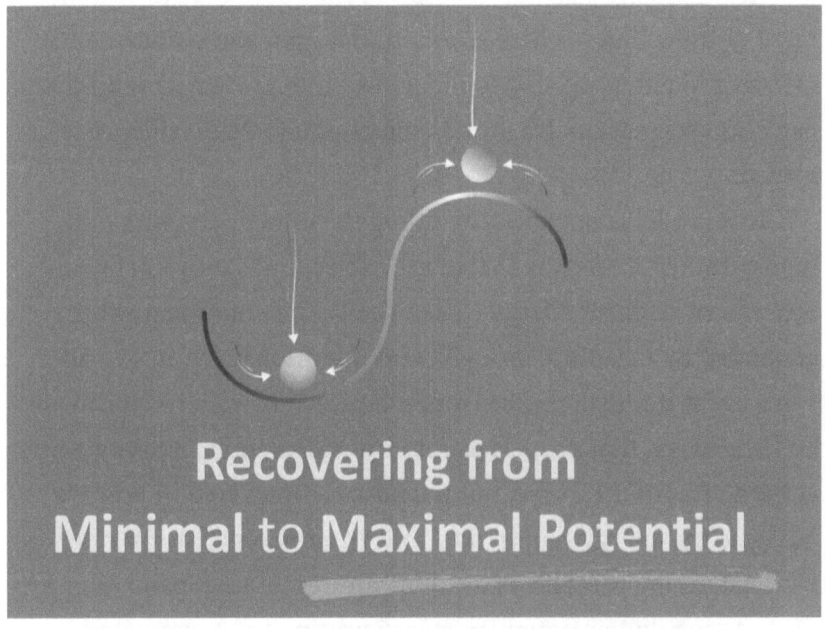

Recovering from Minimal to Maximal Potential

The image presented here illustrates a dynamic model of potential energy as it relates to human emotional states and the process of resilience. Each curved section represents a valley or peak—symbolic of low and high emotional potential. The spheres represent an individual's emotional position at any given moment. Notably, the downward arrows above each sphere reflect the universal pressures of life—the constant forces we all experience, regardless of where we find ourselves emotionally or situationally.

When a person is in a low potential state, they may feel stuck, fatigued, or emotionally inert. While this valley may feel heavy, it's also a place of emotional stability—a resting point where movement is possible. Conversely, a high potential state often reflects emotional vitality, momentum, and elevated performance. Yet even here, stability can become precarious, especially when energy is depleted or adversity strikes.

The "unstable state" at the crest of the curve illustrates a moment of inflection—where emotion, thought, and circumstance intersect to either tip someone forward into growth or send them back into stagnation. It's in these pivot points that resilience is forged.

This model is not about avoiding the lows or clinging to the highs. Rather, it teaches us that growth requires movement, and movement requires energy—specifically, the emotional energy generated by meaning, thought, and intentional action. An adverse event can dislodge us from emotional inertia, but it can also be the catalyst that propels us into transformation. Stability exists at both ends of the curve, but purpose is discovered in how we navigate the energy required to shift from one state to another. Understanding this allows us to reframe emotional pain—not as dysfunction, but as potential energy waiting to be converted into purposeful momentum.

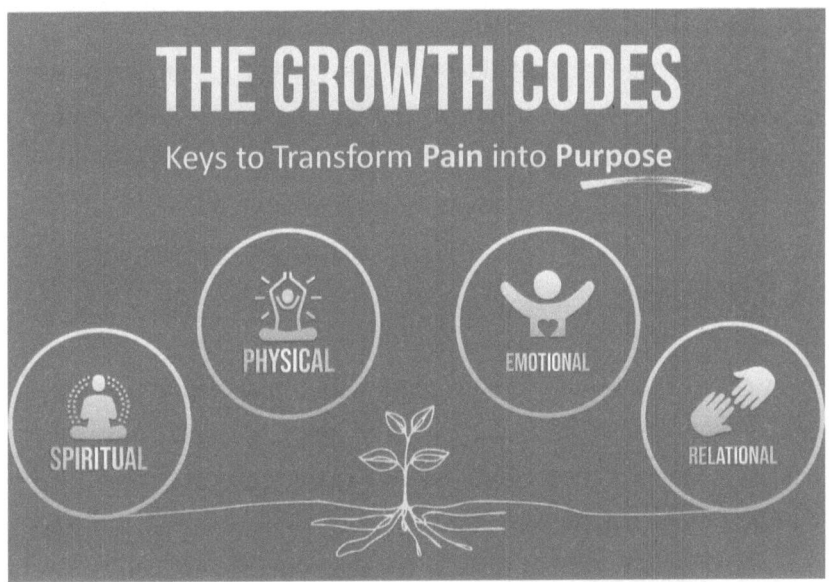

What follows is a description of the four areas of Growth Codes: the spiritual, the physical, the emotional and the relational. A continuum represents each of them. As the reader, you are asked to ponder on each code. As you go through them, I encourage you to take stock of where you are in terms of proficiency. Tell me which codes you feel you've mastered and which ones you know in which you have room to grow. It takes persistence to develop any of the Growth Codes, yet we can all benefit from them. The sections that require more investment are initially denied. Try not to compare yourself to other people; in fact; being truthful will help you considerably. Everyone has their own unique timeline, goals and journey to follow. The potential of one individual is distinct from that of another. To add insult to injury, our first impressions of other people are often prejudiced. Rather, I suggest you reflect on who you are and what you know about the world right now. Acknowledge your current situation and be grateful that there is still more for you to learn. Keep in mind that you may always improve your skills and knowledge. Having a growth mindset means you fully believe that you can and will improve yourself. No matter how difficult things may appear right now, I encourage you to utilize them as motivation to push yourself farther toward resilience. The goal is to make you stronger and longer lasting.

My personal research and life experiences, as well as my many years of client work and involvement with many health-care programs, went into creating the Growth Codes. It is normal practice in the therapeutic profession to consider the connectivity of the mental/emotional, physical, and spiritual aspects. The significance of the interpersonal ties must also be recognized. To reach our maximum resilience potential, we must tend to all these areas of our lives. Our personal and professional environments shape our personal development. Our mental and social well-being are affected when we are physically sick. Our mental and physical health can be affected by unhealthy relationships as well. Even in the absence of material possessions, we can discover the greatest satisfaction in life when we learn to align ourselves with everything.

The Spiritual Growth Code

Of all the domains, the spiritual one is the one talked about most often and is least understood. The essence of who we are can get lost because we are limited to what we can see and touch. Our five physical senses – taste, touch, hear, smell and see – don't detect everything around us. Many people will say that they believe in spirituality. In most cases, this indicates that individuals have an awareness of a spiritual presence or existence. This is where some people put phenomena that no one can explain. Attending a religious ceremony according to one's denomination or tradition is one way that some people practice spirituality. Just as your emotional experiences exist within you that others cannot plainly see, so does your spirit. For the sake of this discourse, embrace the notion that you are a unique spirit with a potential that drives you.

Where energy becomes momentum is in your spirit, which is the core of your creative force. It is like a car's gas tank: it takes in energy in the form of potential and turns it into the force that propels you ahead. In the realm of the spirit, the abstract becomes form, ideas come to life, and the real becomes palpable. Your creative endeavors, whether they be musical compositions, dances, or architectural designs, are all driven by this spiritual energy. To decipher the Spiritual Growth Code, which describes the inner workings of our minds, hearts, and wills, it is necessary to acknowledge the presence of one's spirit.

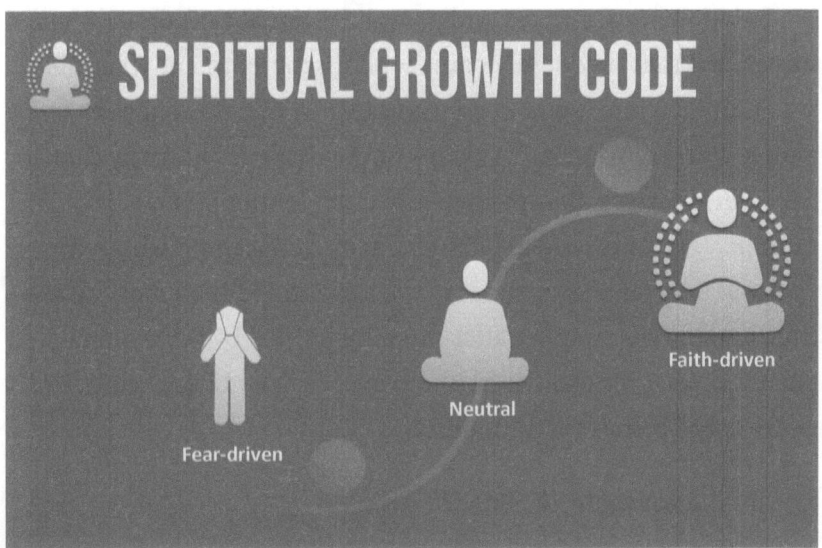

Fear vs. Faith

Do you let faith or fear motivate you more? The Spiritual Growth Code, like all Growth Codes, is non-specific: it ranges from faith-driven action to fear-driven action, with a neutral between ground. The secret to resilience is making the progressive transition from acting out of fear to acting out of faith, even if fear is a normal and even helpful survival mechanism.

When you let your fears dictate your actions, you'll never get what you "do" desire. Motives fueled by fear might masquerade as efficiency. Think about some instances:

- The fear of being alone drives some people to seek out relationships.
- Some people strive for achievement so they can escape the embarrassment of failing.
- Many people try to amass money because they are afraid of being poor.

Relationships, success and prosperity are not necessarily bad things, but they frequently come with discontentment when they are attained while living in constant fear. When this happens, people start to wonder, "Why am I not satisfied?" In many cases, the solution lies in the spiritual aspect of development. A lack of humility, gratitude and delight characterizes accomplishments motivated by fear, in contrast to the former. Feeling empty all the time and always running after or being hunted by an imaginary enemy is what it means to be motivated by fear. Living a life driven by dread brings no tranquility.

Spiritual Alignment: A Potent Force

Finding contentment and fulfillment, no matter how difficult the circumstances, is possible when our deeds are in harmony with our beliefs and goals. Unbeknown to them, many people let their fears dictate their daily lives, preventing them from reaching their greatest potential. Even though they seem to be doing well on the outside, their minds are constantly racing with "what if" scenarios: what if I mess up, what if I fall behind, or what if I never succeed? This fear and worry does create a drive, however, it can be a never-ending race that runs past the goal of purpose into perpetual pain.

Having a faith-driven spirit, on the other hand, releases us from this state of never-ending nervousness. A faith-driven person is receptive to change and views adversity as a chance to grow. Their determination stems from a sense of meaning rather than just surviving. Every action, choice and relationship is impacted by this quiet confidence that spreads outward, fostered by this transformation from fear to faith.

Awakening to the Influence of Pause

Making room for pause is a powerful tool for moving your focus from fear to faith. A state of neutrality is sometimes imposed upon us by life. We are reminded that growth often necessitates stillness by events such as job loss, abrupt sorrow, or even something like the global standstill of the Covid-19 pandemic. During these pauses, we refocus, examine our reasons, and reacquaint ourselves with a purpose that is rooted in our faith.

Acting based on faith means doing it not because we are afraid of the consequences, but because we genuinely want to create, connect and make a difference. Embracing faith instead of fear gives us the strength to persevere through tough times and accomplish our goals with direction and purpose instead of feeling pressured by time. This type of energy may be nurtured and laid the groundwork for long-term, satisfying development; this is what the Spiritual Growth Code is all about.

Overcoming Fear with Faith

Change begins with awareness. Once we become more conscious of what is driving us, we can then begin to shift our mindset. With these questions in mind, I ask you to pause and put yourself in **neutral** before moving forward.

1. *Asking yourself, "Am I acting out of faith or fear?" on a regular basis will help you pause and reflect. Writing down in your journal the times when your faith or fear was the driving force behind your decisions could help you understand them better.*

2. *Stop acting out of fear if you discover that your thoughts are driven by fear. Consider whether this anxiety is based on actual danger or merely a habit. Swap out "I must do this to prevent failure" for "I desire to do this to aid in my development."*

Trust in yourself, your values, and your goal will contain faith-driven energy, which is why it's important to reaffirm your purpose. To deepen this sense of purpose, let your faith lead you when you engage in disciplines such as communication, fitness, work and relationships. Any thought, feeling, or activity can be transformed into something meaningful by enhancing your perspective, as invited to do so in the Spiritual Growth Code. A deeper, more durable resilience—one that brings you peace, pleasure, and fulfillment—can be realized when you progressively shift from a fear-driven attitude to one driven in faith. Faith can thrive in the impossible, but fear will always flee.

The Code for Spiritual Growth: Self-Examination

In your spiritual processes, use these questions to gauge your current level of fear, neutrality or faith. Find out how your inner motivation affects your resilience and general health by reflecting seriously and thoughtfully on the matter.

Spirit Assessment:

1. *Your "spirit" or latent creative ability — how would you describe it?*

2. *In your day-to-day existence, how significant is spirituality or a feeling of purpose?*

3. *Is there a part of you that longs to be a part of something — a faith, a community, the universe — that is bigger than you?*

4. *When you act, how frequently do you consider the feelings (be they fear, faith or habit) that drive you?*

Recognizing Behavior Driven by Fear: Fear

1. *Is fear of rejection, scarcity, or failure a common motivator for your actions?*

2. *Is fear a major factor in your relationships, at work and in achieving your own goals?*

3. After overcoming a fear-based obstacle, do you feel empty or dissatisfied?

4. When you're afraid of something, how do you deal with the "enemies" you imagine lurking around every corner?

Finding a Balance: Being Neutral

1. Is there anything in your life that makes you feel "stuck" or unmotivated, rather than pushed by faith or fear?

2. When was the last time you felt spiritually at peace and grounded?

3. Is it disengagement, tranquility or something else that you associate with the word "neutrality"?

4. Once you realize you need to grow or take action, how do you break out of your neutral state?

Belief: Nurturing Deeds Motivated by Faith

1. Do you make decisions and pursue goals based on a foundation of trust, hope and faith?

2. How can you establish a connection with your faith or inner strength through certain activities like prayer, meditation or gratitude?

3. What effect does acting on faith instead of fear have on your relationships, aspirations and state of mind generally?

4. *Do you feel happiness and contentment in the things that you accomplish or make because of your faith?*

Self-Renewal and Strength

1. *In the face of adversity, what fears did you have to overcome and what faith did you muster?*

2. *For you, is facing hardship more of a setback than a chance to grow spiritually?*

3. *What are some ways that you incorporate the lessons that you've learned from challenges into daily spiritual routine?*

4. *How do you feel about uncertainty? Do you have faith in it or do you run away from it?*

Psycho-Physical-Spiritual Link

1. *How can you find inner peace through exercise, deep breathing or practicing mindfulness?*

2. *Are you cognizant of the fact that your mental and bodily health are influenced by your spiritual well-being?*

3. *When you feel disconnection, what methods do you use to bring your body, mind and soul into harmony?*

Progress and Harmony

1. *Where do you find yourself occupying the majority of your time on the spectrum of Fear, Neutrality, and Faith today?*

2. To what extent do you let your worries prevent you from living a life guided by your faith?

3. How does spiritual growth manifest in your life? How does it help you create joy, find serenity and live intentionally?

4. If you were to make a change in your faith, how would it affect your strength and capacity to deal with adversity?

After you've answered these questions, for each stage, choose one thing you can do:
- Fear: *Is there anything you can intentionally let go of this week that is based on fear?*
- Neutral: *How can one avoid being complacent while embracing balance and pausing?*
- Faith: *How can you build your faith and fortitude through the cultivation of certain practices or beliefs?*

Write, review and read your responses out loud. Remember that the sound of your voice is an instrument of energy. As much as possible, use it to help overtake negative and fretful thought patterns that might pull you back. Bringing yourself to a neutral place is more beneficial than the strain of fear — even though it feels like activation. Learn how to get more comfortable with being still. It is in these moments when you can listen more effectively to your spirit and begin to move more toward faith. Sometimes we need to simply trust that we are okay and safe in this moment.

NOTES

The Code for Physical Development

Your mental and spiritual well-being can take a serious hit when you deal with any kind of disease, no matter how little. Having a common cold or flu can feel like a serious disruption in our systems. Also, having to rely on other people for support while we're physically sick can put a burden on our relationships and our capacity to operate. Undoubtedly, there is a strong link between the mind and the body. If we can learn to relax our bodies, we will be able to bring more composure to our emotional minds. Prolonged health problems, on the other hand, have the potential to change our perspective, chip away at our sense of identity, and exacerbate emotional difficulties like depression, which is frequently associated with long-term sickness.

The goal of the Physical Growth Code, as a code for growth, is to make people more resilient. It encourages us to proactively cultivate resilience by leading us along a continuum of three stages: *Retreat, Rest, Press.*

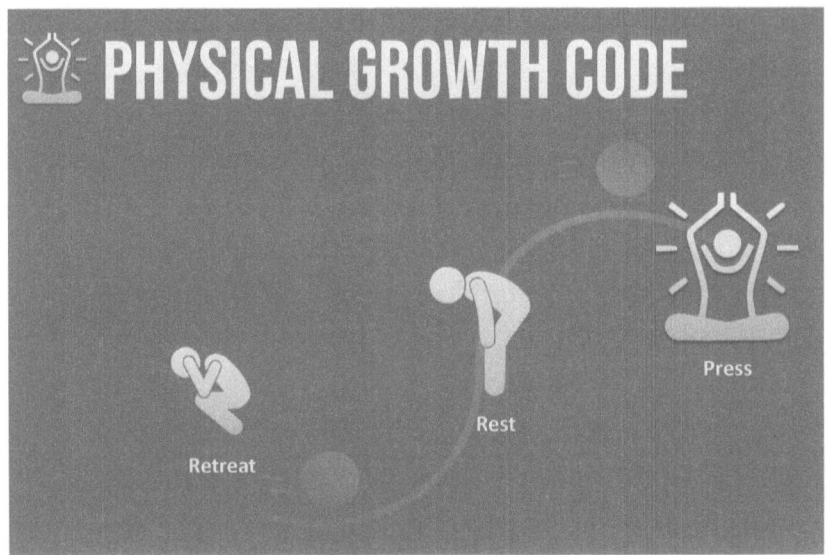

Retreat: Physical Avoidance

Among the worst decisions we can make, leading a sedentary lifestyle greatly increases the risk of obesity, cardiovascular disease and general physical deterioration. Physical effort is limited or even avoided in a retreat phase of the Physical Growth Code. It may be only useful when we are in a deep state of physical illness. This state is not healthy to operate in if we are looking for longevity or quality of life. It can be triggered by several things like fear, exhaustion, or a lack of drive.

Inactivity and lack of motivation to carry out daily tasks are common symptoms of clinical depression. It is important to rule out physical causes when diagnosing depressed persons by looking for signs of disturbed eating, poor sleep, and decreased motivation. As part of treatment, doctors and therapists often recommend exercise, even if the patient doesn't want to do it. Putting our bodies in motion can help cue our mental framework when we are sitting in a lull of minimum potential. The goal is to create movement in the body to help shift the mind and spirit into a higher place.

Why? The reason being, motion gives birth to life. Getting regular exercise helps alleviate sadness, boosts mood and reestablishes a feeling of identity. Movement is fundamental to our physiology. Like a rubber band that gets weak and snaps when stretched too far, a sedentary body can't handle the stresses of daily life and will struggle more during times of hardship.

When you feel like you need to escape, check in with yourself to see if you're really trying to avoid doing anything. Do you try to move your body daily? Getting out of physical retreat is the starting point for building resilience.

Often-Neglected Rest

In today's fast-paced society, the second phase of the Physical Growth Code — **Rest** — is frequently neglected. Taking time out to relax on purpose is essential for recharging your batteries and restoring your energy. Our physical bodies have limitations that we must attend to. We are designed to need regular sleep, hydration, sunlight and proper nutrition.

Relaxation extends beyond the bed. The key is to set aside time on purpose to relax your body and mind. Getting enough sleep gives us the energy to overcome our present situation and get ready for future progress. Rest is the bedrock of resiliency, yet it's a fading art. All our bodily systems, including our neurological, muscular and cognitive systems, need it to heal and restore. Today we live in a sleep-deprived culture. We promote staying up all night for enjoyment and staying up late to work. We caffeinate ourselves into consciousness and see sleep as something reserved for the weak. Remember that you exist in a physical body with a unique rhythm. Part of your design requires rest.

Press Release

Finally, in the Press phase of the Physical Growth Code, we consciously challenge ourselves to our physical limitations for predetermined durations. To get the most out of our bodies, pressing requires us to tune into their natural rhythm.

Intentional movement is essential to the daily rhythms of our bodies, which govern our heart rate, digestion, hunger and sleep cycles. Lifting weights, jogging, dancing or any other physically demanding activity that raises these rhythms is what we need to do while we're in press mode. Discovering movements that work for your energies and objectives is crucial.

There is a direct correlation between moving your body and energizing your thoughts. To stimulate our bodies and drive them to greater levels of performance, we utilize our mental attention and energy throughout exercise. In reaction to potential danger, this activation can occur automatically. Our adrenaline levels rise, our pulse rates quicken and our muscles tense up in anticipation of movement.

Mastering the art of relaxation is equally crucial as is learning to engage our muscles. A regulated breathing pattern and purposeful activity might assist in calming the nervous system and reestablishing equilibrium. You can also find it difficult to utilize your body as a tool for relaxation if you aren't used to pressing it on a regular basis. For this reason, the Physical Code's oscillation between rest and press is crucial.

Strength and stamina aren't the sole benefits of exercise; it also helps with the mind-body connection. This synchronization, like riding a bike, becomes automatic with experience. If you remember when you were a kid, you probably needed some help and maybe even training wheels to learn how to ride a bike. After you find your balance and speed it becomes easy. Just like how steering, accelerating and braking become second nature after some practice, driving a car first requires focus. The mind and body are hardwired to work in tandem; so even when we face in a new but similar challenge we can adjust rapidly.

How to Stay Strong

Intentionally pressing on a regular basis will train you and your body to deal with the challenges that life throws at you. The ability to physically and mentally withstand and recover from adversity is known as resilience. One way to build resilience is to learn to move with purpose and to tune into your body's natural rhythms.

Learning how the Physical Growth Code's three phases — Retreat, Rest, and Press — interact is the key to building resilience. Each stage has a specific purpose:

- The desire for change is signaled by *retreat,* which alerts us to inaction and stagnation.
- Recovery and long-term growth are both supported by *rest.*
- By challenging ourselves to our limits, *press* training increases our stamina and strength.

You can improve your health and mental toughness and pave the way for success in all aspects of your life by getting a handle on these stages. Achieve strength you never thought possible by moving purposefully, resting purposefully, and pushing yourself to your limits. It takes consistency and discipline. It can be beneficial to work with a coach or a person of positive influence to hold us accountable as we build it into a habit — just like the learning phase of riding a bike.

Assessing Oneself: The Physical Development Code

Take stock of where you are on the Retreat, Rest, and Press continuum and where you want to go by asking yourself these questions. To understand your physical level and readiness for resilience, it is important to reflect honestly:

1. How active are you are right now? Do you tend to be very active, somewhat active, or not at all active most of the time?

2. Is getting up and moving about a regular part of your day? What kinds of things do you usually do while you're free?

3. In what ways does the state of your body affect the state of your mind and emotions?

4. How does your body make you feel? Are you able to tell when it needs to move, relax, or recuperate? And, what are the signals to adjust up or down?

Get Away: Acknowledging Vacancy

1. Even when you're aware of the benefits, do you still put off getting moving? If so, for what reason?

2. Is your flexibility, stamina, or strength decreasing as a result of your lack of exercise?

3. Are you presently coping with obstacles that hinder your physical or mental activity, such as fear, illness or a lack of time?

4. How does your mood and energy level change when you don't exercise?

Recuperation Assessment: Rest

1. When you work out, do you make time to relax?

2. How often do you get a good night's sleep and take breaks during the day?

3. Are you feeling rejuvenated and ready to take on the world, or exhausted and drained, after a day of physical exertion?

4. When you take a break, is it something you struggle with, or can you accept as an essential component of personal development?

Press: Pushing Your Boundaries

1. Is increasing your strength and stamina something you do on purpose? In that case, how frequently and through what means?

2. How often do you take time to exercise, even when you don't feel like it?

3. When faced with physical difficulties or stresses, do you

believe in your capacity to handle them?

4. *How effectively do you manage to challenge yourself while also giving your body the rest it needs?*

Connecting Mind and Body

1. *Are you aware of the physical manifestations of stress, such as a racing heart or tense muscles?*

2. *Do you know any methods to relax your nervous system, like yoga or deep breathing?*

3. *When you move, how frequently do you try to bring your thoughts into harmony with your body?*

Thoughts on Progress and Harmony

1. *Where do you find yourself occupying the most of your time on the spectrum between Retreat, Rest and Press?*

2. *Is there anything that is preventing you from progressing further down the continuum?*

3. *What if we make some minor adjustments to the Physical Growth Code so that it becomes more balanced?*

4. *In what ways (if any) will your relationships, profession, mental health and overall well-being be affected by your efforts to increase your physical resilience?*

After you've answered these questions, choose one thing you can do to help create the shift your body requires most:

Retreat: *What's one thing you can do to get out of your lull?*

Rest: *What steps can you take to better your routine for rest and recuperation?*

Press: This week, think of a strategy to deliberately push your body. Write down what you are going to different each day for two weeks.

The Physical Growth Code is the most tangible of all. It is evident in observation how much movement you make each day. You can see how much energy is stored in your body and your musculature based on how it appears. You can see and test how flexible your body is. You can see how much weight you can lift day after day. You can check your heart rate and blood pressure. There are many ways to verify your physical resilience. If you want to lift your level of resilience, the more active and mobile body is more likely going to be able to endure hardship. Start to pace your rhythm each day. If you are unsure on where to start or how to get better consult with your physician for guidance.

NOTES

The Emotional Growth Code

Many people find that emotions are divisive. There tends to be a cultural prejudice that favors suppressing emotions over expressing them when someone is characterized as "emotional," which is often taken negatively. Stoicism is a badge of honor for many people, and they often go to extreme measures to hide their feelings. But the reality is that our emotions are the best tools for experiencing and expressing life. Emotions link us to our inner selves, our social circles and the external environment.

Experiencing emotions together strengthens relationships. Emotions allow us to form bonds that can endure a lifetime, whether it's through shared grief or through laughter until you cry. All humans have common emotional energy, which connects us to the natural world and, by extension, to all living things.

Improving your capacity to form and maintain connections, especially when faced with challenges, is central to the Emotional Growth Code. One of the most important components of resilience is learning to recognize and experience one's own emotions. Recognizing and embracing our emotions as useful tools for personal and professional development is the first step toward developing emotional intelligence, which is increasingly seen as crucial for success in both realms.

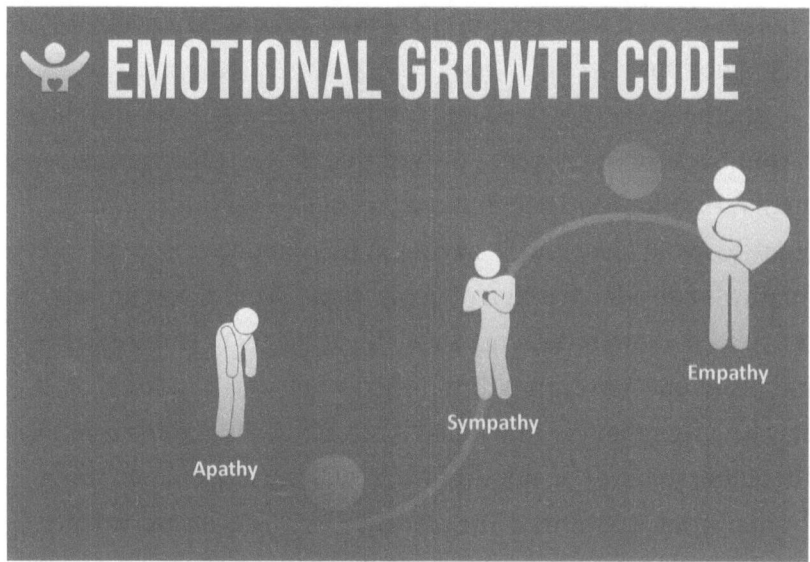

Apathy, Sympathy and Empathy: A Scale for Emotional Growth

From *apathy* to *sympathy* and finally *empathy*, the Emotional Growth Code crosses a range. With each passing stage, we become more in tune with our feelings and better able to communicate, share, and channel those feelings in a way that promotes growth, resilience and healing.

Desensitization to Feelings: Apathy

When people are emotionally detached, they act indifferent — as if nothing is important. This is called apathy. Imagine a teen simply shrugging their shoulders and declaring, "I don't care." They display a lack of interest in anything, tuning out their environment, and stop caring about everything that matters. Mind you this display however is typically not true. It is used as a protective defense, or the individual doesn't have the tools to express emotion or even their environment may feel unsafe to express their emotions.

Apathetic states lack energy for drive and may exhibit feelings of numbness or indifference toward themselves, other people, and their surroundings. Though it may seem like a protective technique to avoid discomfort, staying in this condition is quite risky. Apathy is considered a sign of depression. Depression clinically is considered a lowered energy state. The capacity to endure stress and overcome hardship is diminished when one is indifferent. It may be a sign that the individual is already feeling overwhelmed. Therefore, we must be mindful when making judgements about the appearance of others. The objective here is to examine yourself in a caring manner and from that vantage point begin to see others more clearly.

Neglecting self-care and withdrawing from others are consequences of chronic indifference, which heightens feelings of loneliness and hopelessness. One must reawaken a feeling of care — for oneself, for other people, or for something bigger to overcome apathy.

Self-Examination of Indifference

1. *Have you ever felt like nobody cared whether you were sick or not?*

2. *Describe what happened that made you feel emotionally distant.*

3. *When you don't care, how does it impact your resilience and social skills?*

4. *Find something or someone to care about again; even if it's just a little, who or what would It be?*

Awakening Care: Sympathy

The initial stride away from indifference is sympathy. The capacity to care for another person or animal, a connection that states, "I feel for you," typically develops in response to external motivators like taking care of a youngster, a pet, or a loved one.

A lifeline for many is sympathy. "I couldn't let my dog go hungry." or "I keep going because my children need me." These thoughts demonstrate the strength of empathy in rescuing us from emotional distancing. We discover a little more meaning when we are sympathetic to the condition of others.

Caring for oneself is another invitation from sympathy, albeit it may be difficult. People frequently tell us not to "feel sorry for yourself," which could make us feel bad about ourselves and make us neglect our own needs. Still, the key to recovery and resiliency is practicing self-compassion, which means letting ourselves experience a needed sorrow and tend to our emotional wounds.

Self-Examination of Sympathy

1. *Who or what is the person that means the most to you?*

2. *How does taking care of other people affect your mood and your feeling of meaning in life?*

3. *In what ways can you empathize with yourself without passing judgment?*

4. In what ways could being more compassionate to yourself improve your capacity to care?

Understanding and Sharing Emotions

The pinnacle of emotional intelligence is empathy. To put it simply, it's being able to put yourself in another person's shoes and experience their feelings while keeping your own self grounded. Being empathetic calls for inner fortitude, perseverance and self-awareness.

With empathy, you can let out sorrow when you're unhappy, laughter when you're happy and an embrace when love is close by. You react honestly to the situation by letting your emotions flow freely. When you can put yourself in another person's shoes, you achieve emotional alignment, which in turn strengthens your relationships and makes you more resilient.

True empathy starts with knowing oneself. Realizing your own limitations and validating the difficulty you are experiencing in a given time period. When you work on developing self-empathy, you'll be better able to provide others with unconditional, non-projected compassion. If you don't have it, trying to empathize with other people could come out as insincere or forced. Or you may find yourself always offering fixes rather than being present with someone's pain — including your own.

A strong measure of emotional intelligence — which is closely related to resilience — is empathy, according to researcher Marc Brackett (2018). Instead of repressing or misinterpreting our feelings, emotionally intelligent people can process and adjust to new situations by making sense of them.

Questions for Self-Reflection on Empathy

1. *Do you have no problem expressing yourself, even when you're feeling difficult emotions like anger or sadness?*

2. *How do you handle other people's emotions? Do you empathize, distance yourself or respond?*

3. *Can you think of a time when you really put yourself in another person's shoes?*

4. *If you can't empathize with yourself, how can you expect other people to?*

Feelings as a Source of Vitality and Empowerment

Instead of viewing our emotions as liabilities, the Emotional Growth Code encourages us to view them as resources, either to be expressed or repressed. Misalignment, disorientation, and even problems with physical or mental health can result from suppressing emotions for an extended period. Connection, growth and resilience are fostered via the truthful expression of emotions.

Emotional emergence in this Code entails progress along a continuum: coming from a place of apathy and complete detachment to sympathy, where love awakens and then to where genuine connection and strength flourish — in empathy. You may heal, connect and adjust to life's challenges by accepting your emotions and recognizing their energy. Here are questions to help you examine where you are currently falling along this continuum. I encourage you to write down your answers.

1. *How attuned are you to other people's feelings right now? Are you apathetic, sympathetic, or empathic?*

2. *Do you have any emotional roadblocks that prevent you from forming stronger bonds with other people or with yourself?*

3. *Do you use any methods (such as journaling, therapy or mindfulness) that can assist you in becoming more in tune with and expressive of your emotions?*

A more empathetic version of yourself will allow you to face life's challenges if you work on your emotional development.

NOTES

The Relationship Growth Code

The Relationship Growth Code reflects our interactions with others and the communities we join. To overcome the more difficult challenges in life, having strong relationships is essential. These relationships offer the emotional support and companionship that one needs. People are made to be connected. The human spirit can experience profound anguish and can develop trauma because of being neglected, outcast or abandoned.

We are here to make a difference in the world, to connect with others and to co-create experiences that empower us. While relationships lay the groundwork for development and recovery, they also reveal weaknesses that, when addressed, can strengthen resilience. *Attachment → Isolation → Connection* is the progression along which this Growth Code functions. You can cultivate deeper connections and progress in your personal life by learning your relationship navigating style and where you fit on this spectrum.

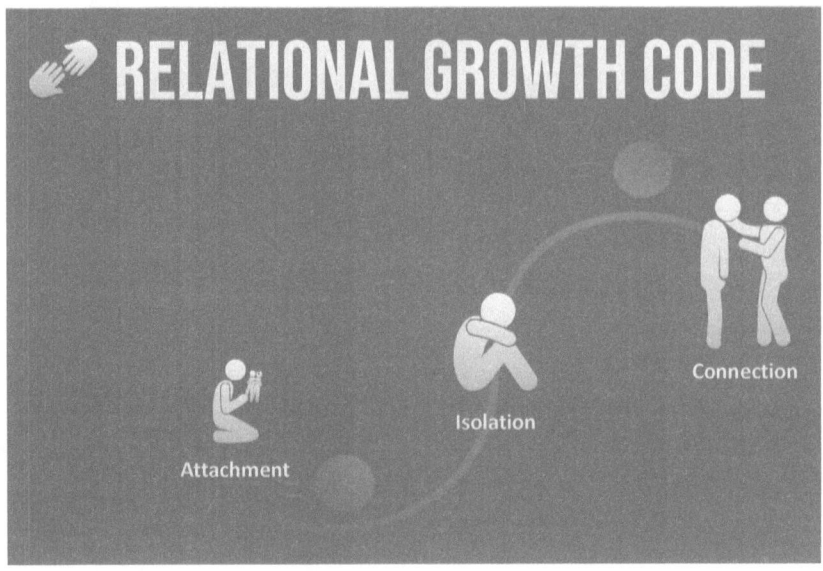

Attachment for Protection

The most basic and fundamental type of relationships are those based on attachment. During this time, you will be looking for someone else's approval, safety, and security more than anything else. During this phase, people frequently have strong emotional reactions such as anger, sadness, or terror when separated from their partners because they feel incomplete or insecure without them.

According to psychotherapist John Bowlby, caregiver interactions in early infancy influence attachment types. When we are small children, our emotional and physical needs are mostly met by our parents or guardians. Attachment patterns like anxious or avoidant styles can persist into adult relationships because of these demands being poorly addressed or not met at all. These experiences shape the development of our nervous system and its ability to regulate a sense of safety.

As an example, when two people are going through a difficult breakup, they tend to blame the other person. The emotional scars are reopened in their nervous systems and usually existed before the couple ever started dating. During close relationships, these wounds become apparent as insecurities, trust issues and sense of belonging come to surface. Because of our attachment, we are unable to perceive the relationship objectively. All we can feel is the breaking of our heart. Even if the connection is unhealthy, it clings on still, even when it hurts.

This is attachment. It is blind and innocent. It has the temperament of a child in pain. Here are some thought-provoking questions to raise your awareness to that child.

1. *Is there someone whom you rely on too much for emotional*

support?

2. When things were bad in a relationship, did you ever decide to stay? If so, what did you overlook to remain with the person?

3. What commonalities do you see between your early relationships and your more recent ones?

4. When you're in a committed relationship, how do you deal with being apart from that person?

Being Alone: Revisiting My Identity

According to the Relationship Growth Code, an important step out of attachment is *isolation*. This may sound like a bad thing, but it's about developing a relationship with yourself and moving away from relying on other people. Learning to be at ease with one's identity apart from the approval of others is a key part of nurturing your own growth. A good way to consider this is to see the process as loving your inner child as though you are re-parenting yourself.

We want to search through our feelings, consider relationships from the past, and discover what patterns come to play. How do these patterns feel like experiences we had in early development? It is an opportunity to get in touch with the inner child (i.e. their emotions) during this phase. Meditation, writing in a notebook, talking to a therapist and spending quality time alone can all help on this path. Facing repressed emotions is a common component of attachment healing. Loneliness, grief and vulnerability are not weaknesses, but rather energy forms necessary for change and development. Identifying and transforming the ways in which we were mis-parented is critical. Otherwise, we will continue to rely on someone who reminds of our parent to do the same again. We are attracted blindly to the emotional energies of our initial caregivers. We must re-narrate the beliefs we have about ourselves with loving intentions.

Keeping in touch with encouraging friends or a reliable community is just as vital as taking the time to reflect on one's own experiences during this challenging period. Remember this can be done on purpose not just after a breakup where we are torn from an attachment suddenly. Practicing healthy isolation does not imply completely cutting off all social contact; rather, it entails appreciating one's own company while also cultivating meaningful, non-dependent relationships.

Questions for Self-Reflection on Time Alone

1. *Can you handle being alone with your emotions and thoughts?*

2. *What things can you do for yourself to take care of your emotional needs?*

3. *If you could change one thing about your relationship history, what would it be?*

4. *How do you keep supportive relationships alive while also growing as an individual?*

Connection: Partnership for Resilience

At its core, the Relationship Growth Code is all about connection. When you are actively nurturing your emotions, you are more ready to form partnerships that are genuine, stable and promote growth for one another. Synergy, in which two people's strengths complement one another to foster personal development without sacrificing either's uniqueness, lies at the heart of connection.

At this point, the bond between the two people has solidified into one that is characterized by love, trust and respect. When two people are connected, rather than codependent, they can rely on each other while also taking care of themselves emotionally. Each person is valued for who they are. In this connection, love sees clearly and still loves with care, concern and nurturing.

When our connections are aligned, they let us accept and be accepted completely. We become more robust and capable when our relationships are built on the foundation of unconditional love. With their help, we can establish reasonable limits, have honest conversations and make lasting memories. A foundation for increased resilience and fulfillment is formed in connection — where we are most empowered to love ourselves and our neighbors.

Connection Questions

1. *Who are the current people in your life that contribute to your development and who are those that hold you back?*

2. *In a partnership, how do you convey your emotions and ideas?*

3. Can you establish and maintain appropriate limits with other people without losing your sense of self?

4. If you were to describe the ideal relationship, what would it look like?

5. In what ways can you create that ideal relationship with yourself?

A Resilience-Based Application of the Relational Growth Code

Your connection with yourself is at the heart of the Relationship Growth Code. To progress the continuum, one must be willing to be vulnerable, patient and compassionate toward oneself.

Acknowledge the underlying needs that motivate your connections and start the process of self-awareness when in Attachment. Focus on tending to your inner child and working through any unresolved emotions while you're in isolation. In Connection, it's important to approach relationships with authenticity, forming bonds that promote personal development and strength. In these relationships, you feel safe when you allow your *inner-child* to be cared for by the other and vice versa without abandoning yourself for their affection or attempting to earn it. Thoughtfully answer these questions to raise your awareness on areas that need more nurturing.

1. On the attachment, isolation or connection spectrum, where do you find yourself right now?

2. If you want to improve your connection with yourself, what can you do?

3. To what extent does your present network mirror your development in this area?

4. How would you characterize resilience in your relationships? In what ways do they make you more durable and it what ways are you more vulnerable in the relationship?

A profound awareness of oneself is the foundation for all meaningful relationships, as the Relationship Growth Code points out. We may strengthen our relationships and our resilience by purposefully navigating through the phases of this continuum. The goal is to move away from attachment into connection. Remember that this transition is less about them than it about your emotional ability to be aware; to convey and care for your energetic needs. When two people are in connection with each other they will discover a synergic rhythm that will enable them both to feel loved and empowered.

NOTES

How Time Contributes to Resilience

In addition to the Growth Codes, our relationship with time becomes a key factor in building and maintaining resilience. The essence of time impacts the course of our life: it controls everything. We can't make it go faster or slower. Time is an essential component of personal growth and resilience because of this certainty.

What makes the passage of time so intriguing is not that it happens, but rather how we perceive it. When we're really into something, time seems to pass quickly, and we say things like, "Time flies!" On the flip side, when things get boring or tough, everything goes very slow, and we start to question if it will ever end. These individual perceptions of time show that although we have no power over the passage of time, we do have control over how we choose to perceive and experience it.

Time as a Structure for Recuperation and Development

"Time heals all wounds" and "Time will tell" are two popular proverbs that highlight the need of waiting for healing to take place or for a truth to be revealed. Though time doesn't actively alleviate suffering or provide insight, time provides a structure within which we can digest, adapt, develop and discover. The sum of all our Earth-related revolutions and orbits that make up our age and is more than just a number; it is a window into our journey on this planet. Every time the Earth goes around the sun, it gives us a new opportunity to learn and adapt.

Time is a neutral entity; it advances regardless of our conditions. Our reactions to the experiences time gives us are within our control. The way we spend our days, or the quality of our rotations, is determined by how we value our relationship with time. To make the most of these rotations, it is necessary to strengthen one's mind, body and soul. This is what gives us a better quality of life. The value we ascribe to time is enhanced when our relationships with ourselves, others and God (or a higher power) are strengthened. At the end of life, we want to sense the quality of and the quantity of time we experienced making connections with our purposes — to know that our life has had meaning.

Giving up to the Pressures of Resilience

Learning to let go and let time take its course is one of life's biggest obstacles. The passing of time causes a great deal of anxiety and tension for many of us, when we begin see it as an adversary that must be overcome or chased. Time, on the other hand, can be viewed as a valuable ally, a commodity necessary for progress. The virtue of patience teaches us to be still and unmoved by the passing of time, which is essential to building resilience. It sets a mindset that enables us to be present in the moment and to value the connections with things around us.

The ability to wait for something we want, exercise restraint and find inner calm is what we mean when we talk of patience as a virtue. Being patient and not trying to force things can help us to overcome obstacles and come out stronger. The mental space necessary for growth and healing can be achieved by viewing time as a companion rather than an adversary.

Resilience, Dynamics, and Time

Entropy, which stands for the slow disintegration or disorder of things over time, is one example of an irreversible process associated with time from a scientific viewpoint. In terms of resilience, this indicates that inefficient or unadaptable systems are more likely to fail when faced with adversity.

To overcome this innate propensity for disorder, we need to work on establishing harmony and order in our own systems, which include our thoughts, emotions, physical selves and interpersonal connections. Disorganization and a lack of resilience are worsened by toxic factors including bad habits, toxic relationships or flawed mental frameworks.

It is vital that you channel your focus into aligning these realms. Resilience isn't just about getting through tough times; it's about thriving in the face of adversity, learning from your mistakes and becoming more self-actualized.

You can use the Growth Codes as a framework to better understand yourself, evaluate your current state of being and unlock your full potential. Strengthening one's resilience takes time and effort. It takes time and effort to cultivate any of the four areas outlined by the Growth Codes: physical, emotional, relational and spiritual. Use time in conjunction with each of these codes and you will find increased resilience and continued growth with deepening and expanded purposes.

Your efforts are multiplied by time:
- Wisdom is cultivated by constant learning and awareness.
- Taking care of your body is a certain way to boost your energy and power.
- Harmony and direction are yours when you get in touch with your spirit.
- Meaning and connection are found through the cultivation of loving relationships.

Living in the Passage of Time

Let's examine further how the ways you perceive time influence how you experience life. Do you see it as an adversary, and you race against it to reach your objectives? On the other hand, do you view it as a companion who can help you evolve and progress?

1. *What are you doing with your life right now, and does it support your objectives and values?*

2. *When faced with adversity, do you try to fight against the passage of time or welcome it as a tool for getting better?*

3. *Is your experience with time being eroded by any harmful influences, whether they be habits, relationships or thoughts?*

4. *In what ways can the Growth Codes (Spiritual, Physical, Emotional or Relational) help you structure your efforts and goals according to the passage of time?*

Among our most precious resources is time. Possibilities for resilience, fulfillment and change arise when we figure out how to use maximize time, rather than rush or avoid it. Every revolution, every orbit presents an opportunity for personal growth — one moment at a time.

NOTES

Grow into Purpose

The journey from pain into purpose is done by way of resilience. There must be energy released for you to transform into who you were meant to be. Don't let adversity push you away from your destiny. Look into and through it. Find the reworking necessary through the tension. Everything is within you, but it must be cultivated with time. All your external experiences can help shape you into what you can become. You are not what happened to you, but you become what's transmitted through you. You can transform negative into positive. Prepare yourself with resilience within and your hope will be realized.

"Never let a good crisis go to waste." This quote, often attributed to Winston Churchill during World War II, carries a powerful insight — one that hinges on the word *good*. Reframing a crisis as an opportunity rather than a catastrophe is how we activate resilience.

Crisis is a point of momentum — a crossroads where transformation becomes possible. When I served as the director of a mental health crisis center, I initially loathed the word *crisis*. At one point, I even advocated for changing the department's name to avoid the negative connotation. The stigma surrounding mental health treatment troubled me, and I believed that *emergency* was a more neutral, all-encompassing term for moments of distress.

But over time, experience reshaped my perspective. I came to see crisis not as a threat, but as a catalyst for change. Crisis is the pivot point: the moment of impact that forces a shift. It doesn't mean the experience isn't painful or overwhelming, but within that breaking, there is energy — an energy that, if harnessed, can propel us forward with even greater force. When we learn to lean into crisis rather than recoil from it, we discover its hidden potential: the power to transform, to rebuild and to emerge stronger than before.

"I think, therefore I am," famously proclaimed the French philosopher René Descartes. His insight that *being* is based on thinking rather than sensations alone highlights the influence of the mind in molding reality. The energy you possess most powerfully manifests in your thoughts. In the end, they determine how resilient you are, how you organize your inner world and how you perceive time.

Your beliefs and the way you live your life will be a direct reflection of your sense of purpose in life. You will actively seek out, share and feel love if you truly believe you are deserving of it. The first step toward building resilience is changing the way you think about yourself and how you see yourself moving through the world regardless of what it tries to deceive you with. You are loved and valued.

Both mentally and physically, I've grown stronger today compared to yesterday. Having discovered my life's true calling and taking steps to cultivate it, I am now prepared to take on the challenges and seize the opportunities that come my way on this purpose-driven path. It takes inner strength as much as it does outside power to walk in unison with one's purpose.

As a fellow adventurer on this incredible journey, I offer you this encouragement. Keep going ahead without fear. You will achieve greatness through your determined persistence, and you will gain wisdom through your submission to Spirit. Know each day that you are loved for who you are and protected for who you are meant to be.

References

Brackett, M. A. (2018). The emotional intelligence we owe students and educators. Educational Leadership, 76 (2), 1218.

Dell'Osso, L., Lorenzi, P., Nardi, B., Carmassi, C., & Carpita, B. (2022). Post Traumatic Growth (PTG) in the Frame of Traumatic Experiences. *Clinical neuropsychiatry, 19*(6), 390–393. https://doi.org/10.36131/cnfioritieditore20220606

Carver, C.S, Scheier, M.F, & Segerstrom, S.C. (2010). Optimism. Clinical Psychology Review, 30(7), 879889.

Che SE, Gwon YG, Kim K. Follow-Up Timing After Discharge and Suicide Risk Among Patients Hospitalized With Psychiatric Illness. *JAMA Netw Open.* 2023;6(10):e2336767. doi:10.1001/jamanetworkopen.2023.36767

Connor, K. M., & Davidson, J. R. (2003). Development of a new resilience scale: The Connor-Davidson resilience scale (CD-RISC). *Depression and anxiety,* 18(2), 76-82

Joseph, V. A., Martinez-Ales, G., Olfson, M., Shaman, J., Gould, M. S., Gimbrone, C., & Keyes, K. M. (2023). Trends in suicide among Black women in the United States, 1999–2020. *American Journal of Psychiatry, 180*(12), 914–917.

Knipscheer, J., Sleijpen, M., Frank, L., de Graaf, R., Kleber, R., Ten Have, M., & Dückers, M. (2020). Prevalence of Potentially Traumatic Events, Other Life Events and Subsequent Reactions

Indicative for Posttraumatic Stress Disorder in the Netherlands: A General Population Study Based on the Trauma Screening Questionnaire. *International journal of environmental research and public health*, *17*(5), 1725. https://doi.org/10.3390/ijerph17051725

Lock, S., Rees, C. S., & Heritage, B. (2020). Development and validation of a brief measure of psychological resilience: The state–trait assessment of resilience scale. *Australian Psychologist*, 55(1), 10-25

Rollins, M. R. & Cross. T, L. (2014) A Deeper Investigation Into the Psychological Changes of Intellectually Gifted Students Attending a Residential Academy, Roeper Review, 36:1, 1829, DOI: 10.1080/02783193.2014.856372

Rollins, M. R., & Cross, T. L. (2014). Assessing the Psychological Changes of Gifted Students Attending a Residential High School With an Outcome Measurement. Journal for the Education of the Gifted, 37(4), 337354. https://doi.org/10.1177/0162353214552562

Smith, B. W., Dalen, J., Wiggins, K., Tooley, E., Christopher, P., & Bernard, J. (2008). The brief resilience scale: assessing the ability to bounce back. *International journal of behavioral medicine*, 15(3), 194-200

Van Bael, K., Ball, M., Scarfo, J., & Suleyman, E. (2023). Assessment of the mindbody connection: preliminary psychometric evidence for a new self-report questionnaire. *BMC psychology*, *11*(1), 309. https://doi.org/10.1186/s40359023013023

NOTES

NOTES

NOTES

Want to discover your resilience strengths?

Scan this QR code to take the
Growth Code Assessment — a quick
5-minute self-check to uncover insights about
your habits, mindset, and resilience.

Unlock your personal growth journey today!

www.ingramcontent.com/pod-product-compliance
Lightning Source LLC
Chambersburg PA
CBHW022058120526
44580CB00017B/128/J